Deep Learning with PyTorch Quick Start Guide

Learn to train and deploy neural network models in Python

David Julian

BIRMINGHAM - MUMBAI

Deep Learning with PyTorch Quick Start Guide

Copyright © 2018 Packt Publishing

Commissioning Editor: Amey Varangaonkar
Acquisition Editor: Noyonika Das
Content Development Editor: Kirk Dsouza
Technical Editor: Sushmeeta Jena
Copy Editor: Safis Editing
Project Coordinator: Hardik Bhinde
Proofreader: Safis Editing
Indexer: Mariammal Chettiyar
Graphics: Alishon Mendonsa
Production Coordinator: Nilesh Mohite

First published: December 2018

Production reference: 1201218

Published by Packt Publishing Ltd.
Livery Place
35 Livery Street
Birmingham
B3 2PB, UK.

ISBN 978-1-78953-409-2

www.packtpub.com

`mapt.io`

Mapt is an online digital library that gives you full access to over 5,000 books and videos, as well as industry leading tools to help you plan your personal development and advance your career. For more information, please visit our website.

Why subscribe?

- Spend less time learning and more time coding with practical eBooks and Videos from over 4,000 industry professionals

- Improve your learning with Skill Plans built especially for you

- Get a free eBook or video every month

- Mapt is fully searchable

- Copy and paste, print, and bookmark content

Packt.com

Did you know that Packt offers eBook versions of every book published, with PDF and ePub files available? You can upgrade to the eBook version at `www.packt.com` and as a print book customer, you are entitled to a discount on the eBook copy. Get in touch with us at `customercare@packtpub.com` for more details.

At `www.packt.com`, you can also read a collection of free technical articles, sign up for a range of free newsletters, and receive exclusive discounts and offers on Packt books and eBooks.

Contributors

About the author

David Julian is a freelance technology consultant and educator. He has worked as a consultant for government, private, and community organizations on a variety of projects, including using machine learning to detect insect outbreaks in controlled agricultural environments (Urban Ecological Systems Ltd., Bluesmart Farms), designing and implementing event management data systems (Sustainable Industry Expo, Lismore City Council), and designing multimedia interactive installations (Adelaide University). He has also written *Designing Machine Learning Systems With Python* for Packt Publishing and was technical reviewer for *Python Machine Learning* and *Hands-On Data Structures and Algorithms with Python - Second Edition*, published by Packt.

About the reviewer

AshishSingh Bhatia has more than 10 years' IT experience in different domains, including ERP, banking, education, and resource management. He is a learner, reader, and developer at heart. He is passionate about Python, Java, and R. He loves to explore new technologies. He has also published two books: *Machine Learning with Java and R* and *Natural Language Processing with Java*. Apart from this, he has also recorded a video tutorial on PyTorch.

Packt is searching for authors like you

If you're interested in becoming an author for Packt, please visit `authors.packtpub.com` and apply today. We have worked with thousands of developers and tech professionals, just like you, to help them share their insight with the global tech community. You can make a general application, apply for a specific hot topic that we are recruiting an author for, or submit your own idea.

Table of Contents

Preface   1

Chapter 1: Introduction to PyTorch   7
What is PyTorch?   8
Installing PyTorch   10
   Digital Ocean   12
     Tunneling in to IPython   13
   Amazon Web Services (AWS)   14
Basic PyTorch operations   14
   Default value initialization   15
   Converting between tensors and NumPy arrays   16
   Slicing and indexing and reshaping   19
   In place operations   21
Loading data   22
   PyTorch dataset loaders   24
     Displaying an image   26
     DataLoader   26
     Creating a custom dataset   27
     Transforms   29
   ImageFolder   30
   Concatenating datasets   31
Summary   31

Chapter 2: Deep Learning Fundamentals   33
Approaches to machine learning   34
Learning tasks   35
   Unsupervised learning   36
     Clustering   36
     Principle component analysis   36
     Reinforcement learning   37
   Supervised learning   37
     Classification   37
     Evaluating classifiers   38
Features   39
   Handling text and categories   40
Models   41
   Linear algebra review   41
   Linear models   45
     Gradient descent   47
     Multiple features   50
     The normal equation   51

Logistic regression	51
Nonlinear models	54
Artificial neural networks	55
The perceptron	56
Summary	60
Chapter 3: Computational Graphs and Linear Models	61
autograd	62
Computational graphs	64
Linear models	65
Linear regression in PyTorch	65
Saving models	69
Logistic regression	70
Activation functions in PyTorch	72
Multi-class classification example	73
Summary	79
Chapter 4: Convolutional Networks	81
Hyper-parameters and multilayered networks	81
Benchmarking models	83
Convolutional networks	88
A single convolutional layer	88
Multiple kernels	90
Multiple convolutional layers	91
Pooling layers	91
Building a single-layer CNN	92
Building a multiple-layer CNN	94
Batch normalization	96
Summary	98
Chapter 5: Other NN Architectures	99
Introduction to recurrent networks	99
Recurrent artificial neurons	100
Implementing a recurrent network	101
Long short-term memory networks	107
Implementing an LSTM	110
Building a language model with a gated recurrent unit	111
Summary	117
Chapter 6: Getting the Most out of PyTorch	119
Multiprocessor and distributed environments	119
Using a GPU	120
Distributed environments	122
torch.distributed	122
torch.multiprocessing	123
Optimization techniques	124
Optimizer algorithms	124

Learning rate scheduler   126
Parameter groups   127
Pretrained models   129
Implementing a pretrained model   131
Summary   136

Other Books You May Enjoy   139

Index   143

Preface

PyTorch is surprisingly easy to learn and provides advanced features such as a supporting multiprocessor, as well as distributed and parallel computation. PyTorch has a library of pre-trained models, providing out-of-the-box solutions for image classification. PyTorch offers one of the most accessible entry points into cutting-edge deep learning. It is tightly integrated with the Python programming language, so for Python programmers, coding it seems natural and intuitive. The unique, dynamic way of treating computational graphs means that PyTorch is both efficient and flexible.

Who this book is for

This book is for anyone who wants a straightforward, practical introduction to deep learning using PyTorch. The aim is to give you an understanding of deep learning models by direct experimentation. This book is perfect for those who are familiar with Python, know some machine learning basics, and are looking for a way to productively develop their skills. The book will focus on the most important features and give practical examples. It assumes you have a working knowledge of Python and are familiar with the relevant mathematical ideas, including with linear algebra and differential calculus. The book provides enough theory to get you up and running without requiring rigorous mathematical understanding. By the end of the book, you will have a practical knowledge of deep learning systems and able to apply PyTorch models to solve the problems that you care about.

What this book covers

Chapter 1, *Introduction to PyTorch*, gets you up and running with PyTorch, demonstrates its installation on a variety of platforms, and explores key syntax elements and how to import and use data in PyTorch.

Chapter 2, *Deep Learning Fundamentals*, is a whirlwind tour of the basics of deep learning, covering the mathematics and theory of optimization, linear networks, and neural networks.

Chapter 3, *Computational Graphs and Linear Models*, demonstrates how to calculate the error gradient of a linear network and how to harness it to classify images.

Chapter 4, *Convolutional Networks*, examines the theory of convolutional networks and how to use them for image classification.

Chapter 5, *Other NN Architectures*, discusses the theory behind recurrent networks and shows how to use them to make predictions about sequence data. It also discusses **long short-term memory networks (LSTMs)** and has you build a language model to predict text.

Chapter 6, *Getting the Most out of PyTorch*, examines some advanced features, such as using PyTorch in multiprocessor and parallel environments. You will build a flexible solution for image classification using out-of-the-box pre-trained models.

To get the most out of this book

This book does not assume any specialist knowledge, only solid general computer skills. Python is a relatively easy (and incredibly useful!) language to learn, so don't worry if you have limited or no programming background.

The book does contain some relatively simple mathematics, and some theory, that some readers may find difficult at first. Deep learning models are complex systems and understanding the behavior of even simple neural networks is a non-trivial exercise. Fortunately, PyTorch acts as a high-level framework around these complicated systems, so it is possible to achieve very good results without an expert understanding of the theoretical foundations.

Installing the software is easy, and essentially only two packages are required: the Anaconda distribution of Python, and PyTorch itself. The software runs on Windows 7 and 10 , macOS 10.10 or above, and most versions of Linux. It can be run on a desktop machine or in a server environment. All the code in this book was tested using PyTorch version 1.0 and Python 3, running on Ubuntu 16.

Download the example code files

You can download the example code files for this book from your account at www.packt.com. If you purchased this book elsewhere, you can visit www.packt.com/support and register to have the files emailed directly to you.

You can download the code files by following these steps:

1. Log in or register at `www.packt.com`.
2. Select the **SUPPORT** tab.
3. Click on **Code Downloads & Errata**.
4. Enter the name of the book in the **Search** box and follow the onscreen instructions.

Once the file is downloaded, please make sure that you unzip or extract the folder using the latest version of:

- WinRAR/7-Zip for Windows
- Zipeg/iZip/UnRarX for Mac
- 7-Zip/PeaZip for Linux

The code bundle for the book is also hosted on GitHub at `https://github.com/PacktPublishing/Deep-Learning-with-PyTorch-Quick-Start-Guide`. In case there's an update to the code, it will be updated on the existing GitHub repository.

We also have other code bundles from our rich catalog of books and videos available at `https://github.com/PacktPublishing/`. Check them out!

Download the color images

We also provide a PDF file that has color images of the screenshots/diagrams used in this book. You can download it here: `https://www.packtpub.com/sites/default/files/downloads/9781789534092_ColorImages.pdf`.

Conventions used

There are a number of text conventions used throughout this book.

`CodeInText`: Indicates code words in text, database table names, folder names, filenames, file extensions, pathnames, dummy URLs, user input, and Twitter handles. Here is an example: "Mount the downloaded `WebStorm-10*.dmg` disk image file as another disk in your system."

A block of code is set as follows:

```
import numpy as np
x = np.array([[1,2,3],[4,5,6],[1,2,5]])
y = np.linalg.inv(x)
print (y)
print (np.dot(x,y))
```

When we wish to draw your attention to a particular part of a code block, the relevant lines or items are set in bold:

```
import numpy as np
x = np.array([[1,2,3],[4,5,6],[1,2,5]])
y = np.linalg.inv(x)
print (y)
print (np.dot(x,y))
```

Bold: Indicates a new term, an important word, or words that you see onscreen. For example, words in menus or dialog boxes appear in the text like this. Here is an example: "Select **System info** from the **Administration** panel."

Warnings or important notes appear like this.

Tips and tricks appear like this.

Get in touch

Feedback from our readers is always welcome.

General feedback: If you have questions about any aspect of this book, mention the book title in the subject of your message and email us at customercare@packtpub.com.

Errata: Although we have taken every care to ensure the accuracy of our content, mistakes do happen. If you have found a mistake in this book, we would be grateful if you would report this to us. Please visit www.packt.com/submit-errata, selecting your book, clicking on the Errata Submission Form link, and entering the details.

Piracy: If you come across any illegal copies of our works in any form on the Internet, we would be grateful if you would provide us with the location address or website name. Please contact us at copyright@packt.com with a link to the material.

If you are interested in becoming an author: If there is a topic that you have expertise in and you are interested in either writing or contributing to a book, please visit authors.packtpub.com.

Reviews

Please leave a review. Once you have read and used this book, why not leave a review on the site that you purchased it from? Potential readers can then see and use your unbiased opinion to make purchase decisions, we at Packt can understand what you think about our products, and our authors can see your feedback on their book. Thank you!

For more information about Packt, please visit packt.com.

Introduction to PyTorch 1

This is a step-by-step introduction to deep learning using the PyTorch framework. PyTorch is a great entry point into deep learning and if you have some knowledge of Python then you will find PyTorch an intuitive, productive, and enlightening experience. The ability to rapidly prototype experiments and test ideas is a core strength of PyTorch. Together with the possibility of being able to turn experiments into productive, deployable resources, the learning curve challenge is abundantly rewarded.

PyTorch is a relatively easy and fun way to understand deep learning concepts. You may be surprised at how few lines of code it takes to solve common problems of classification, such as hand-writing recognition and image classification. Having said that PyTorch is *easy* cannot override the fact that deep learning is, in many ways, *hard*. It involves some complicated math and some intractable logical conundrums. This should not, however, distract from the fun and useful part of this enterprise. There is no doubt machine learning can provide deep insights and solve important problems in the world around us but to get there can take some work.

This book is an attempt, not to gloss over important ideas, but to explain them in a way that is jargon free and succinct. If the idea of solving complicated differential equations makes you break out in a cold sweat, you are not alone. This might be related to some high school trauma of a bad-tempered math teacher furiously demanding you cite Euler's formula or the trigonometric identities. This is a problem because math itself should be fun, and insight arises not from the laborious memorizing of formulas but through understanding relationships and foundational concepts.

Another thing that can make deep learning appear difficult is that it has a diverse and dynamic frontier of research. This may be confusing for the novice because it does not present an obvious entry point. If you understand some principles and want to test your ideas, it can be a bewildering task to find a suitable set of tools. The combinations of development language, framework, deployment architecture, and so on, present a non-trivial decision process.

The science of machine learning has matured to the point that a set of general purpose algorithms for solving problems such has classification and regression have emerged. Subsequently, several frameworks have been created to harness the power of these algorithms and use them for general problem solving. This means that the entry point is at such a level that these technologies are now in the hands of the non-computer science professional. Experts in a diverse array of domains can now use these ideas to advance their endeavors. By the end of this book, and with a little dedication, you will be able to build and deploy useful deep learning models to help solve the problems you are interested in.

In this chapter, we will discuss the following topics:

- What is PyTorch?
- Installing PyTorch
- Basic operations
- Loading data

What is PyTorch?

PyTorch is a dynamic tensor-based, deep learning framework for experimentation, research, and production. It can be used as a GPU-enabled replacement for NumPy or a flexible, efficient platform for building neural networks. The dynamic graph creation and tight Python integration makes PyTorch a standout in deep learning frameworks.

If you are at all familiar with the deep learning ecosystem, then frameworks such as Theano and TensorFlow, or higher-level derivatives such as Keras, are amongst the most popular. PyTorch is a relative newcomer to the deep learning framework set. Despite this, it is now being used extensively by Google, Twitter, and Facebook. It stands out from other frameworks in that both Theano and TensorFlow encode computational graphs in static structures that need to be run in self-contained sessions. In contrast, PyTorch can dynamically implement computational graphs. The consequence for a neural net is that the network can change behavior as it is being run, with little or no overhead. In TensorFlow and Theano, to change behavior, you effectively have to rebuild the network from scratch.

This dynamic implementation comes about through a process called tape-based auto-diif, allowing PyTorch expressions to be automatically differentiated. This has numerous advantages. Gradients can be calculated on the fly and since the computational graph is dynamic, it can be changed at each function call, allowing it to be used in interesting ways in loops and under conditional calls that can respond, for example, to input parameters or intermediate results. This dynamic behavior and great flexibility has made PyTorch a favored experimental platform for deep learning.

Another advantage of PyTorch is that it is closely integrated with the Python language. For Python coders, it is very intuitive and it interoperates seamlessly with other Python packages, such as NumPy and SciPy. PyTorch is very easy to experiment with. It makes an ideal tool for not only building and running useful models, but also as a way to understand deep learning principles by direct experimentation.

As you would expect, PyTorch can be run on multiple **graphical processing units** (**GPUs**). Deep learning algorithms can be computationally expensive. This is especially true for big datasets. PyTorch has strong GPU support, with intelligent memory sharing of tensors between processes. This basically means there is an efficient and user-friendly way to distribute the processing load across the CPU and GPUs. This can make a big difference to the time it takes to test and run large complex models.

Dynamic graph generation, tight Python language integration, and a relatively simple API makes PyTorch an excellent platform for research and experimentation. However, versions prior to PyTorch 1 had deficits that prevented it from excelling in production environments. This deficiency is being addressed in PyTorch 1.

Research is an important application for deep learning, but increasingly, deep learning is being embedded in applications that run live on the web, on a device, or in a robot. Such an application may service thousands of simultaneous queries and interact with massive, dynamic data. Although Python is one of the best languages for humans to work with, specific efficiencies and optimizations are available in other languages, most commonly C++ and Java. Even though the best way to build a particular deep learning model may be with PyTorch, this may not be the best way to deploy it. This is no longer a problem because now with PyTorch 1, we can export Python free representations of PyTorch models.

This has come about through a partnership between Facebook, the major stakeholder of PyTorch, and Microsoft, to create the **Open Neural Network Exchange** (**ONNX**) to assist developers in converting neural net models between frameworks. This has led to the merging of PyTorch with the more production-ready framework, CAFFE2. In CAFFE2, models are represented by a plain text schema, making them language agnostic. This means they are more easily deployed to Android, iOS, or Rasberry Pi devices.

With this in mind, PyTorch version 1 has expanded its API included production-ready capabilities, such as optimizing code for Android and iPhone, a **just in time** (JIT) C++ compiler, and several ways to make *Python free* representations of your models.

In summary, PyTorch has the following characteristics:

- Dynamic graph representation
- Tightly integrated with the Python programming language
- A mix of high-and low-level APIs
- Straightforward implementation on multiple GPUs
- Able to build *Python-free* model representation for export and production
- Scales to massive data using the Caffe framework

Installing PyTorch

PyTorch will run on macOS X, 64 bit Linux, and 64 bit Windows. Be aware that Windows does not currently offer (easy) support for the use of GPUs in PyTorch. You will need to have either Python 2.7 or Python 3.5 / 3.6 installed on your computer before you install PyTorch, remembering to install the correct version for each Python version. Unless you have a reason not to, it is recommended that you install the Anaconda distribution of Python. This this is available from: `https://anaconda.org/anaconda/python`.

Anaconda includes all the dependencies of PyTorch, as well as technical, math, and scientific libraries essential to your work in deep learning. These will be used throughout the book, so unless you want to install them all separately, install Anaconda.

The following is a list of the packages and tools that we will be using in this book. They are all installed with Anaconda:

- `NumPy`: A math library primarily used for working with multidimensional arrays
- `Matplotlib`: A plotting and visualization library
- `SciPy`: A package for scientific and technical computing
- `Skit-Learn`: A library for machine learning
- `Pandas`: A library for working with data
- `IPython`: A notebook-style code editor used for writing and running code in a browser

Once you have Anaconda installed, you can now install PyTorch. Go to the PyTorch website at `https://pytorch.org/`.

The installation matrix on this website is pretty self-explanatory. Simply select your operating system, Python version, and, if you have GPUs, your CUDA version, and then run the appropriate command.

As always, it is good practice to ensure your operating system and dependent packages are up to date before installing PyTorch. Anaconda and PyTorch run on Windows, Linux, and macOS, although Linux is probably the most used and consistent operating system. Throughout this book, I will be using Python 3.7 and Anaconda 3.6.5 running on Linux

Code in this book was written on the Jupyter Notebook and these notebooks are available from the book's website.

You can either choose to set up your PyTorch environment locally on your own machine or remotely on a cloud server. They each have their pros and cons. Working locally has the advantage that it is generally easier and quicker to get started. This is especially true if you are not familiar with SSH and the Linux terminal. It is simply a matter of installing Anaconda and PyTorch, and you are on your way. Also, you get to choose and control your own hardware, and while this is an upfront cost, it is often cheaper in the long run. Once you start expanding hardware requirements, cloud solutions can become expensive. Another advantage of working locally is that you can choose and customize your **integrated development envionment (IDE)**. In fact, Anaconda has its own excellent desktop IDE called Spyder.

There are a few things you need to keep in mind when building your own deep learning hardware and you require GPU acceleration:

- Use NVIDIA CUDA-compliant GPUs (for example, GTX 1060 or GTX 1080)
- A chipset that has at least 16 PCIe lanes
- At least 16 GB of RAM

Working on the cloud does offer the flexibility to work from any machine as well as more easily experiment with different operating systems, platforms, and hardware. You also have the benefit of being able to share and collaborate more easily. It is generally cheap to get started, costing a few dollars a month, or even free, but as your projects become more complex and data intensive, you will need to pay for more capacity.

Let's look briefly at the installation procedures for two cloud server hosts: Digital Ocean and Amazon Web Services.

Digital Ocean

Digital Ocean offers one of the simplest entry points into cloud computing. It offers predictable simple payment structures and straightforward server administration. Unfortunately, Digital Ocean does not currently support GPUs. The functionality revolves around *droplets*, pre-built instances of virtual private servers. The following are the steps required to set up a droplet:

1. Sign up for an account with Digital Ocean. Go to `https://www.digitalocean.com/`.
2. Click on the **Create** button and choose **New Droplet.**
3. Select the Ubuntu distribution of Linux and choose the two gigabyte plan or above.
4. Select the CPU optimization if required. The default values should be fine to get started.
5. Optionally, set up public/private key encryption.
6. Set up an SSH client (for example, PuTTY) using the information contained in the email sent to you.
7. Connect to your droplet via your SSH client and `curl` the latest Anaconda installer. You can find the address location of the installer for your particular environment at `https://repo.continuum.io/`.
8. Install PyTorch using this command:

```
conda install pytorch torchvision -c pytorch
```

Once you have spun up your droplet, you can access the Linux command through an SSH client. From Command Prompt, you can `curl` the latest Anaconda installer available from: `https://www.anaconda.com/download/#linux`.

An installation script is also available from the continuum archive at `https://repo.continuum.io/archive/`. Full step-by-step instructions are available from the Digital Ocean tutorials section.

Tunneling in to IPython

IPython is an easy and convenient way to edit code through a web browser. If you are working on a desktop computer, you can just launch IPython and point your browser to `localhost:8888`. This is the port that the IPython server, Jupyter, runs on. However, if you are working on a cloud server, then a common way to work with code is to tunnel in to IPython using SSH. Tunneling in to IPython involves the following steps:

1. In your SSH client, set your destination port to `localhost:8888`. In PuTTY, go to **Connection | SSH | Tunnels**.
2. Set the source port to anything above `8000` to avoid conflicting with other services. Click **Add**. Save these settings and open the connection. Log in to your droplet as usual.
3. Start the IPython server by typing `jupyter notebook` into Command Prompt of your server instance.
4. Access IPython by pointing your browser to `localhost: source port`; for example, `localhost:8001`.
5. Start the IPython server.

Note that you may need a token to access the server for the first time. This is available from the command output once you start Jupyter. You can either copy the URL given in this output directly into your browser's address bar, changing the port address to your local source port address, for example: `8001`, or you can elect to paste the token, the part after `token=`, into the Jupyter start-up page and replace it with a password for future convenience. You now should be able to open, run, and save IPython notebooks.

Amazon Web Services (AWS)

AWS is the original cloud computing platform, most noted for its highly-scalable architecture. It offers a vast array of products. What we need to begin is an EC2 instance. This can be accessed form the **Services** tab of the AWS control panel. From there, select **EC2** and then **Launch Instance**. From here, you can choose the machine image you require. AWS provide several types of machine images specifically for deep learning. Feel free to experiment with any of these but the one we are going to use here is the deep learning AMI for Ubuntu version 10. It comes with pre-installed environments for PyTorch and TensorFlow. After selecting this, you get to choose other options. The default T2 micro with 2 GB of memory should be fine to experiment with; however, if you want GPU acceleration, you will need to use the T2 medium instance type. Finally, when you launch your instance, you will be prompted to create and download your public-private key pair. You can then use your SSH client to connect to the server instance and tunnel in to the Jupyter Notebook as per the previous instructions. Once again, check the documentation for the finer details. Amazon has a pay-per-resource model, so it is important you monitor what resources you are using to ensure you do not receive any unnecessary or unexpected charges.

Basic PyTorch operations

Tensors are the workhorse of PyTorch. If you know linear algebra, they are equivalent to a matrix. Torch tensors are effectively an extension of the numpy.array object. Tensors are an essential conceptual component in deep learning systems, so having a good understanding of how they work is important.

In our first example, we will be looking at tensors of size 2 x 3. In PyTorch, we can create tensors in the same way that we create NumPy arrays. For example, we can pass them nested lists, as shown in the following code:

```
In [5]:    1  import torch
           2
           3  x= torch.tensor([[1,2,3],[4,5,6]])
           4  y= torch.tensor([[7,8,9], [10,11,12]])
           5
           6  f= 2*x + y
           7  print f

tensor([[  9,  12,  15],
        [ 18,  21,  24]])
```

Here we have created two tensors, each with dimensions of 2 x 3. You can see that we have created a simple linear function (more about linear functions in Chapter 2, *Deep Learning Fundamentals*) and applied it to x and y and printed out the result. We can visualize this with the following diagram:

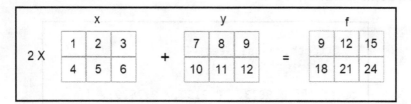

As you may know from linear algebra, matrix multiplication and addition occur element-wise so that for the first element of *x*, let's write this as X_{00}. This is multiplied by two and added to the first element of *y*, written as Y_{00}, giving $F_{00} = 9$. $X_{01} = 2$ and $Y_{01} = 8$ so $f_{01} = 4 + 12$. Notice that the indices start at zero.

If you have never seen any linear algebra, don't worry too much about this, as we are going to brush up on these concepts in Chapter 2, *Deep Learning Fundamentals*, and you will get to practice with Python indexing shortly. For now, just consider our 2 x 3 tensors as tables with numbers in them.

Default value initialization

There are many cases where we need to initialize torch tensors to default values. Here, we create three 2 x 3 tensors, filling them with zeros, ones, and random floating point numbers:

```
1  shape=[2,3]
2  xzeros =torch.zeros(shape)
3  xones = torch.ones(shape)
4  xrnd = torch.rand(shape)
5  print(xzeros)
6  print(xones)
7  print xrnd
```

```
tensor([[ 0.,   0.,   0.],
        [ 0.,   0.,   0.]])
tensor([[ 1.,   1.,   1.],
        [ 1.,   1.,   1.]])
tensor([[ 0.7104,   0.9464,   0.7890],
        [ 0.2814,   0.7886,   0.5895]])
```

An important point to consider when we are initializing random arrays is the so-called seed of reproducibility. See what happens when you run the preceding code several times. You get a different array of random numbers each time. Often in machine learning, we need to be able to reproduce results. We can achieve this by using a random seed. This is demonstrated in the following code:

```
1 torch.manual_seed(42)
2 print torch.rand([2,3])

tensor([[ 0.8823,  0.9150,  0.3829],
        [ 0.9593,  0.3904,  0.6009]])
```

Notice that when you run this code many times, the tensor values stay the same. If you remove the seed by deleting the first line, the tensor values will be different each time the code is run. It does not matter what number you use to seed the random number generator, as long as it is consistently, achieves reproducible results.

Converting between tensors and NumPy arrays

Converting a NumPy array is as simple as performing an operation on it with a torch tensor. The following code should make this clear:

```
1 import numpy as np
2
3 xnp= np.array([[1,2,3],[4,5,6]])
4 f2= xnp + y
5 print(f2)
6 f2.type()

tensor([[  8,  10,  12],
        [ 14,  16,  18]])

'torch.LongTensor'
```

We can see the result of the type torch tensor. In many cases, we can use NumPy arrays interchangeably with tensors and always be sure the result is a tensor. However, there are times when we need to explicitly create a tensor from an array. This is done with the torch.from_numpy function:

```
1 xtensor = torch.from_numpy(xnp)
2 print(xtensor)
3 print(xtensor.type())
4
```

```
tensor([[ 1,  2,  3],
        [ 4,  5,  6]])
torch.LongTensor
```

To convert from a tensor to a NumPy array, simply call the `torch.numpy()` function:

```
1 print(f.type()) #call the tensors type method
2 fnp = f.numpy() #create aan array from the tensor
3 type(fnp) #uses the python inbuilt type
```

```
torch.LongTensor
```

```
numpy.ndarray
```

Notice that we use Python's built-in `type()` function, as in `type(object)`, rather than the `tensor.type()` we used previously. The NumPy arrays do not have a `type` attribute. Another important thing to understand is that NumPy arrays and PyTorch tensors share the same memory space. For example, see what happens when we change a variables value as demonstrated by the following code:

```
In [80]:   1 a = np.ones(3)
           2 t = torch.from_numpy(a)      #create a tensor from an array
           3 b = t.numpy()                #Create an array from the tensor
           4 b[1] = 0                     #change a value in the array
           5 print(a[1] == b[1])          #this value changes in the original array
           6 print(t)                     # and also in the tensor - they share the same memory

           True
           tensor([ 1.,  0.,  1.], dtype=torch.float64)
```

Note also that when we print a tensor, it returns a tuple consisting of the tensor itself and also its `dtype`, or data type attribute. It's important here because there are certain `dtype` arrays that cannot be turned into tensors. For example, consider the following code:

```
1  int8np=np.ones((2,3),dtype=np.int8)
2  bad= torch.from_numpy(int8np)
```

This will generate an error message telling us that only supported `dtype` are able to be converted into tensors. Clearly, `int8` is not one of these supported types. We can fix this by converting our `int8` array to an `int64` array before passing it to `torch.from_numpy`. We do this with the `numpy.astype` function, as the following code demonstrates:

```
1  good = torch.from_numpy(int8np.astype(np.int32))
2  good.type

'torch.IntTensor'
```

It is also important to understand how `numpy dtype` arrays convert to torch `dtype`. In the previous example, `numpy int32` converts to `IntTensor`. The following table lists the torch `dtype` and their `numpy` equivalents:

Numpy type	dtype	Torch type	Description
int64	torch.int64 torch.float	LongTensor	64 bit integer
int32	torch.int32 torch.int	IntegerTensor	32 bit signed integer
uint8	torch.uint8	ByteTensor	8 bit unsigned integer
float64 double	torch.float64 torch.double	DoubleTensor	64 bit floating point
float32	torch.float32 torch.float	FloatTensor	32 bit floating point
	torch.int16 torch.short	ShortTensor	16 bit signed integer
	torch.int8	CharTensor	6 bit signed integer

The default `dtype` for tensors is `FloatTensor`; however, we can specify a particular data type by using the tensor's `dtype` attribute. For an example, see the following code:

```
1  xint=torch.ones( 2,3 , dtype=torch.int)
2  xint.type()

'torch.IntTensor'
```

Slicing and indexing and reshaping

torch.Tensor have most of the attributes and functionality of NumPy. For example, we can slice and index tensors in the same way as NumPy arrays:

```
1 print(x[0])
2 print(x[1][0:2])

[1 2 3]
[4 5]
```

Here, we have printed out the first element of x, written as x_0, and in the second example, we have printed out a slice of the second element of x; in this case, x_{11} and x_{12}.

If you have not come across slicing and indexing, you may want to look at this again. Note that indexing begins at 0, not 1, and we have kept our subscript notation consistent with this. Notice also that the slice [1][0:2] is the elements x_{10} and x_{11}, inclusive. It excludes the ending index, index 2, specified in the slice.

We can can create a reshaped copy of an existing tensor using the view() function. The following are three examples:

```
1 print(x.view(-1))
2 print(x.view(3,2))
3 print x.view(6,1)

tensor([ 1,  2,  3,  4,  5,  6])
tensor([[ 1,  2],
        [ 3,  4],
        [ 5,  6]])
tensor([[ 1],
        [ 2],
        [ 3],
        [ 4],
        [ 5],
        [ 6]])
```

It is pretty clear what (3,2) and (6,1) do, but what about the –1 in the first example? This is useful if you know how many columns you require, but do not know how many rows this will fit into. Indicating –1 here is telling PyTorch to calculate the number of rows required. Using it without another dimension simply creates a tensor of a single row. You could rewrite example two mentioned previously, as follows, if you did not know the input tensor's shape but know that it needs to have three rows:

```
1 print x.view(3,-1)

tensor([[ 1,  2],
        [ 3,  4],
        [ 5,  6]])
```

An important operation is swapping axes or transposing. For a two-dimensional tensor, we a can use `tensor.transpose()`, passing it the axis we want to transpose. In this example, the original 2 x 3 tensor becomes a 3 x 2 tensor. The rows simply become the columns:

```
1 print x.transpose(0,1)

tensor([[ 1,  4],
        [ 2,  5],
        [ 3,  6]])
```

In PyTorch, `transpose()` can only swap two axes at once. We could use `transpose` in multiple steps; however, a more convenient way is to use `permute()`, passing it the axes we want to swap. The following example should make this clear:

```
1 a = torch.ones(1,2,3,4)
2 print(a.transpose(0,3).transpose(1,2).size())    #swaps axis in two steps
3 print(a.permute(3,2,1,0).size())                  #swaps all axis at once

torch.Size([4, 3, 2, 1])
torch.Size([4, 3, 2, 1])
```

When we are considering tensors in two dimensions, we can visualize them as flat tables. When we move to higher dimensions, this visual representation becomes impossible. We simply run out of spatial dimensions. Part of the magic of deep learning is that it does not matter much in terms of the mathematics involved. Real-world features are each encoded into a dimension of a data structure. So, we may be dealing with tensors of potentially thousands of dimensions. Although it might be disconcerting, most of the ideas that can be illustrated in two or three dimensions work just as well in higher dimensions.

In place operations

It is important to understand the difference between in place and assignment operations. When, for example, we use transpose(x), a value is returned but the value of x does not change. In all the examples up until now, we have been performing operations by assignment. That is, we have been assigning a variable to the result of an operation, or simply printing it to the output, as in the preceding example. In either case, the original variable remains untouched. Alternatively, we may need to apply an operation in place. We can, of course, assign a variable to itself, such as in x = x.transpose(0,1); however, a more convenient way to do this is with in place operations. In general, in place operations in PyTorch have a trailing underscore. For an example, see the following code:

```
1 print(x)
2 x.transpose_(1,0)
3 print x
tensor([[ 1,  2,  3],
        [ 4,  5,  6]])
tensor([[ 1,  4],
        [ 2,  5],
        [ 3,  6]])
```

As another example, here is the linear function we started this chapter with using in place operations on y:

```
1 print y
2 y.add_(x*2)
3 print(y)
```

```
tensor([[  7,   8,   9],
        [ 10,  11,  12]])
tensor([[  9,  12,  15],
        [ 18,  21,  24]])
```

Loading data

Most of the time you will spend on a deep learning project will be spent working with data and one of the main reasons that a deep learning project will fail is because of bad, or poorly understood data. This issue is often overlooked when we are working with well-known and well-constructed datasets. The focus here is on learning the models. The algorithms that make deep learning models work are complex enough themselves without this complexity being compounded by something that is only partially known, such as an unfamiliar dataset. Real-world data is noisy, incomplete, and error prone. These axes of confoundedness mean that if a deep learning algorithm is not giving sensible results, after errors of logic in the code are eliminated, bad data, or errors in our understanding of the data, are the likely culprit.

So putting aside our wrestle with data, and with an understanding that deep learning can provide valuable real-world insights, how do we learn deep learning? Our starting point is to eliminate as many of the variables that we can. This can be achieved by using data that is well known and representative of a specific problem; say, for example, classification. This enables us to have both a starting point for deep learning tasks, as well as a standard to test model ideas.

One of the most well-known datasets is the MNIST dataset of hand-written digits, where the usual task is to correctly classify each of the digits, from zero through nine. The best models get an error rate of around 0.2%. We could apply this well-performing model with a few adjustments, to any visual classification task, with varying results. It is unlikely we will get results anywhere near 0.2% and the reason is because the data is different. Understanding how to tweek a deep learning model to take into account these sometimes subtle differences in data, is one of the key skills of a successful deep learning practitioner.

Consider an image classification task of facial recognition from color photographs. The task is still classification but the differences in that data type and structure dictate how the model will need to change to take this into account. How this is done is at the heart of machine learning. For example, if we are working with color images, as opposed to black and white images, we will need two extra input channels. We will also need output channels for each of the possible classes. In a handwriting classification task, we need 10 output channels; one channel for each of the digits. For a facial recognition task, we would consider having an output channel for each target face (say, for criminals in a police database).

Clearly, an important consideration is data types and structures. The way image data is structured in an image is vastly different to that of, say, an audio signal, or output from a medical device. What if we are trying to classify people's names by the sound of their voice, or classify a disease by its symptoms? They are all classification tasks; however, in each specific case, the models that represent each of these will be vastly different. In order to build suitable models in each case, we will need to become intimately acquainted with the data we are using.

It is beyond the scope of this book to discuss the nuances and subtleties of each data type, format, and structure. What we can do is give you a brief insight into the tools, techniques, and best practice of data handling in PyTorch. Deep learning datasets are often very large and it is an important consideration to see how they are handled in memory. We need to be able to transform data, output data in batches, shuffle data, and perform many other operations on data before we feed it to a model. We need to be able to do all these things without loading the entire dataset into memory, since many datasets are simply too large. PyTorch takes an object approach when working with data, creating class objects for each specific activity. We will examine this in more detail in the coming sections.

PyTorch dataset loaders

Pytorch includes data loaders for several datasets to help you get started. The `torch.dataloader` is the class used for loading datasets. The following is a list of the included torch datasets and a brief description:

MNIST	Handwritten digits 1–9. A subset of NIST dataset of handwritten characters. Contains a training set of 60,000 test images and a test set of 10,000.
Fashion-MNIST	A drop-in dataset for MNIST. Contains images of fashion items; for example, T-shirt, trousers, pullover.
EMNIST	Based on NIST handwritten characters, including letters and numbers and split for 47, 26, and 10 class classification problems.
COCO	Over 100,000 images classified into everyday objects; for example, person, backpack, and bicycle. Each image can have more than one class.
LSUN	Used for large-scale scene classification of images; for example, bedroom, bridge, church.
Imagenet-12	Large-scale visual recognition dataset containing 1.2 million images and 1,000 categories. Implemented with `ImageFolder` class, where each class is in a folder.
CIFAR	60,000 low-res (32 32) color images in 10 mutually exclusive classes; for example, airplane, truck, and car.
STL10	Similar to CIFAR but with higher resolution and larger number of unlabeled images.
SVHN	600,000 images of street numbers obtained from Google Street View. Used for recognition of digits in real-world settings.
PhotoTour	Learning Local Image descriptors. Consists of gray scale images composed of 126 patches accompanied with a descriptor text file. Used for pattern recognition.

Here is a typical example of how we load one of these datasets into PyTorch:

```
1  import torch
2  import torchvision
3  import torchvision.transforms as transforms
4
5  trainset = torchvision.datasets.CIFAR10(root='./data',    #data root directory
6                                                             #The training set
7                                           download=True,    #checks if data has downloaded else does so
8                                           transform = transforms.ToTensor())   #transforms to tensor
9  trainset

Files already downloaded and verified

Dataset CIFAR10
    Number of datapoints: 50000
    Split: train
    Root Location: ./data
    Transforms (if any): ToTensor()
    Target Transforms (if any): None
```

CIFAR10 is a `torch.utils.dataset` object. Here, we are passing it four arguments. We specify a root directory relative to where the code is running, a Boolean, `train`, indicating if we want the test or training set loaded, a Boolean that, if set to `True`, will check to see if the dataset has previously been downloaded and if not download it, and a callable transform. In this case, the transform we select is `ToTensor()`. This is an inbuilt class of `torchvision.transforms` that makes the class return a tensor. We will discuss transforms in more detail later in the chapter.

The contents of the dataset can be retrieved by a simple index lookup. We can also check the length of the entire dataset with the `len` function. We can also loop through the dataset in order. The following code demonstrates this:

```
1  for i in range(len(trainset)):
2      print('size of image {} label {}'.format(trainset[i][0].size() , trainset[i][1]))
3      if i>2: break
size of image torch.Size([3, 32, 32]) label 6
size of image torch.Size([3, 32, 32]) label 9
size of image torch.Size([3, 32, 32]) label 9
size of image torch.Size([3, 32, 32]) label 4
```

Displaying an image

The CIFAR10 dataset object returns a tuple containing an image object and a number representing the label of the image. We see from the size of the image data, that each sample is a 3 x 32 x 32 tensor, representing three color values for each of the 322 pixels in the image. It is important to know that this is not quite the same format used for matplotlib. A tensor treats an image in the format of [color, height, width], whereas a numpy image is in the format [height, width, color]. To plot an image, we need to swap axes using the permute() function, or alternatively convert it to a NumPy array and using the transpose function. Note that we do not need to convert the image to a NumPy array, as matplotlib will display the correctly permuted tensor. The following code should make this clear:

```
1  import matplotlib.pyplot as plt
2  %matplotlib inline
3
4  torchimage=trainset[0][0]     #Indexes the first element of the first tuple ie the 1st image
5  npimage=torchimage.permute(1, 2, 0) #changes the axis C H W to H W C
6  plt.imshow(npimage)    #plots the image - no need to convert to numpy
7
```

```
<matplotlib.image.AxesImage at 0x7f1fa7c594a8>
```

DataLoader

We will see that in a deep learning model, we may not always want to load images one at a time or load them in the same order each time. For this, and other reasons, it is often better to use the torch.utils.data.DataLoader object. DataLoader provides a multipurpose iterator to sample the data in a specified way, such as in batches, or shuffled. It is also a convenient place to assign workers in multiprocessor environments.

In the following example, we sample the dataset in batches of four samples each:

```
1  trainloader = torch.utils.data.DataLoader(trainset, batch_size=4, shuffle=True)
2  dataiter = iter(trainloader)            #create an iterator from a dataloader object
3  images, labels = dataiter.next()        #builds tensors for the images and labels in the batch
4  print(labels[0:])                       #prints the label of the images in the batch
5  print(images.size())                    #prints the size of the batch
```

```
tensor([ 6,  2,  0,  6])
torch.Size([4, 3, 32, 32])
```

Here `DataLoader` returns a tuple of two tensors. The first tensor contains the image data of all four images in the batch. The second tensor are the images labels. Each batch consists of four image label, pairs, or samples. Calling `next()` on the iterator generates the next set of four samples. In machine learning terminology, each pass over the entire dataset is called an epoch. This technique is used extensively, as we will see to train and test deep learning models.

Creating a custom dataset

The `Dataset` class is an abstract class representing a dataset. Its purpose is to have a consistent way of representing the specific characteristics of a dataset. When we are working with unfamiliar datasets, creating a `Dataset` object is a good way to understand and represent the structure of the data. It is used with a `data loader` class to draw samples from a dataset in a clean and efficient manner. The following diagram illustrates how these classes are used:

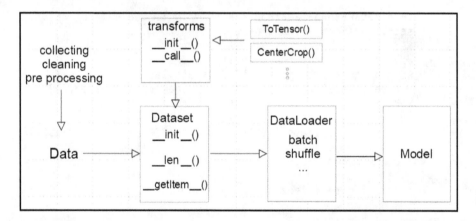

Common actions we perform with a `Dataset` class include checking the data for consistency, applying transform methods, dividing the data into training and test sets, and loading individual samples.

In the following example, we are using a small toy dataset consisting of images of objects that are classified as either toys or not toys. This is representative of a simple image classification problem where a model is trained on a set of labeled images. A deep learning model will need the data with various transformations applied in a consistent manner. Samples may need to be drawn in batches and the dataset shuffled. Having a framework for representing these data tasks greatly simplifies and enhances deep learning models.

The complete dataset is available at `http://www.vision.caltech.edu/pmoreels/Datasets/Giuseppe_Toys_03/`.

For this example, I have created a smaller subset of the dataset, together with a `labels.csv` file. This is available in the `data/GiuseppeToys` folder in the GitHub repository for this book. The class representing this dataset is as follows:

```python
from torch.utils.data import Dataset, DataLoader
from torchvision import transforms
from PIL import Image
import torch
import csv
import os

class toyDataset(Dataset):

    def __init__(self, dataPath, labelsFile,  transform=None):

        self.dataPath=dataPath      #the path to the data directory
        self.transform = transform  #a transform object

        #builds a list of (name,label) tuples
        with open(os.path.join(self.dataPath,labelsFile)) as f:
            self.labels=[tuple(line) for line in csv.reader(f)]
        # checks that all images files exist
        for i in range(len(self.labels)):
            assert os.path.isfile(dataPath + '/' + self.labels[i][0])

    # so we can use dataset.len()
    def __len__(self):
        return len(self.labels)

    #so we can use indexing
    def __getitem__(self, idx):
        imageName,imageLabel=self.labels[idx][0:]
        imagePath =  os.path.join(self.dataPath,imageName)
        image = Image.open(open(imagePath, 'rb'))

        #transforms the image if required
        if self.transform:
            image = self.transform(image)
        return((image,imageLabel))
```

The __init__ function is where we initialize all the properties of the class. Since it is only called once when we first create the instance to do all the things, we perform all the housekeeping functions, such as reading CSV files, setting the variables, and checking data for consistency. We only perform operations that occur across the entire dataset, so we do not download the payload (in this example, an image), but we make sure that the critical information about the dataset, such as directory paths, filenames, and dataset labels are stored in variables.

The __len__ function simply allows us to call Python's built-in len() function on the dataset. Here, we simply return the length of the list of label tuples, indicating the number of images in the dataset. We want to make sure that stays as simple and reliable as possible because we depend on it to correctly iterate through the dataset.

The __getitem__ function is an built-in Python function that we override in our Dataset class definition. This gives the Dataset class the functionality of Python sequence types, such as the use of indexing and slicing. This method gets called often—every time we do an index lookup—so make sure it only does what it needs to do to retrieve the sample.

To harness this functionality into our own dataset, we need to create an instance of our custom dataset as follows:

```
1 toydata = toyDataset('data/GiuseppeToys','labels.csv', transform=transforms.ToTensor())
2 print(toydata[0][0].size()) #the size of the first image in the dataset
3 print(toydata[0][1]) #the label
```

```
torch.Size([3, 551, 816])
 toy
```

Transforms

As well as the ToTensor() transform, the torchvision package includes a number of transforms specifically for Python imaging library images. We can apply multiple transforms to a dataset object using the compose function as follows:

```
1 tforms= transforms.Compose([transforms.Grayscale(3), transforms.CenterCrop(300), transforms.ToTensor()])
2 toyData=toyDataset('data/GiuseppeToys','labels.csv', transform =tforms)
```

Compose objects are essentially a list of transforms that can then be passed to the dataset as a single variable. It is important to note that the image transforms can only be applied to PIL image data, not tensors. Since transforms in a compose are applied in the order that they are listed, it is important that the `ToTensor` transform occurs last. If it is placed before the PIL transforms in the `Compose` list, an error will be generated.

Finally, we can check that it all works by using `DataLoader` to load a batch of images with transforms, as we did before:

```
1 toyloader = DataLoader(toyData, batch_size=4, shuffle=True)
2 toyiter= iter(toyloader)
3 images, labels = toyiter.next()
4 print(labels[0:])
5 print(images.size())

(' notoy ', ' toy ', ' toy', ' toy ')
torch.Size([4, 3, 500, 500])
```

ImageFolder

We can see that the main function of the dataset object is to take a sample from a dataset, and the function of `DataLoader` is to deliver a sample, or a batch of samples, to a deep learning model for evaluation. One of the main things to consider when writing our own dataset object is how do we build a data structure in accessible memory from data that is organized in files on a disk. A common way we might want to organize data is in folders named by class. Let's say that, for this example, we have three folders named `toy`, `notoy`, and `scenes`, contained in a parent folder, `images`. Each of these folders represent the label of the files contained within them. We need to be able to load them while retaining them as separate labels. Happily, there is a class for this, and like most things in PyTorch, it is very easy to use. The class is `torchvision.datasets.ImageFolder` and it is used as follows:

```
1 from torchvision import datasets
2 dataFromFolders = datasets.ImageFolder(root='data/GiuseppeToys/images', transform=tforms)
3 folderloader = DataLoader dataFromFolders, batch_size=4, shuffle=True
4 images, labels = iter(folderloader).next()
5 print(labels)

tensor([ 2,  2,  1,  3])
```

Within the data/GiuseppeToys/images folder, there are three folders, toys, notoys, and scenes, containing images with their folder names indicating labels. Notice that the retrieved labels using DataLoader are represented by integers. Since, in this example, we have three folders, representing three labels, DataLoader returns integers 1 to 3, representing the image labels.

Concatenating datasets

It is clear that the need will arise to join datasets—we can do this with the torch.utils.data.ConcatDataset class. ConcatDataset takes a list of datasets and returns a concatenated dataset. In the following example, we add two more transforms, removing the blue and green color channel. We then create two more dataset objects, applying these transforms and, finally, concatenating all three datasets into one, as shown in the following code:

```
1 cc2,cc3=RemoveChannel('b'), RemoveChannel('g')
2 tforms2=transforms.Compose([transforms.CenterCrop(500), transforms.ToTensor(), cc2])
3 tforms3=transforms.Compose([transforms.CenterCrop(500), transforms.ToTensor(), cc2])
4 toydata2=toyDataset('data/GiuseppeToys','labels.csv', transform =tforms2, train=True)
5 toydata3=toyDataset('data/GiuseppeToys','labels.csv', transform =tforms3, train=True)
6 concatDataset= torch.utils.data.ConcatDataset([toydata,toydata2, toydata3])
7 len(concatDataset)
```

324

Summary

In this chapter, we have introduced some of the features and operations of PyTorch. We gave an overview of the installation platforms and procedures. You have hopefully gained some knowledge of tensor operations and how to perform them in PyTorch. You should be clear about the distinction between in place and by assignment operations and should also now understand the fundamentals of indexing and slicing tensors. In the second half of this chapter, we looked at loading data into PyTorch. We discussed the importance of data and how to create a dataset object to represent custom datasets. We looked at the inbuilt data loaders in PyTorch and discussed representing data in folders using the ImageFolder object. Finally, we looked at how to concatenate datasets.

In the next chapter, we will take a whirlwind tour of deep learning fundamentals and their place in the machine learning landscape. We will get you up to speed with the mathematical concepts involved, including looking at linear systems and common techniques for solving them.

Deep Learning Fundamentals

2

Deep learning is generally considered a subset of machine learning, involving the training of **artificial neural networks** (**ANNs**). ANNs are at the forefront of machine learning. They have the ability to solve complex problems involving massive amounts of data. Many of the principles of machine learning generally are also important in deep learning specifically, so we will spend some time reviewing these here.

In this chapter, we will discuss the following topics:

- Approaches to machine learning
- Learning tasks
- Features
- Models
- Artificial neural networks

Approaches to machine learning

Prior to general machine learning, if we wanted to, for example, build a spam filter, we could start by compiling a list of words that commonly appear in spam. The spam detector then scans each email and when the number of blacklisted words reaches a threshold, the email would be classified as spam. This is called a rules-based approach, and is illustrated in the following diagram:

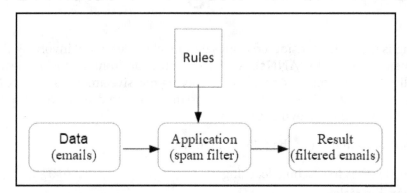

The problem with this approach is that once the writers of spam know the rules, they are able to craft emails that avoid this filter. The people with the unenviable task of maintaining this spam filter would have to continually update the list of rules. With machine learning, we can effectively automate this rule-updating process. Instead of writing a list of rules, we build and train a model. As a spam detector, it will be more accurate since it can analyze large volumes of data. It is able to detect patterns in data that would be impossible for a human to do in a meaningful timeframe. The following diagram illustrates this approach:

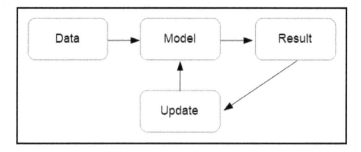

There are a large number of ways that we can approach machine learning and these approaches are broadly characterized by the following factors:

- Whether or not models are trained with labelled training data. There are several possibilities here, including entirely supervised, semi-supervised, based on reinforcement, or entirely unsupervised.
- Whether they are **online** (that is, learning on the fly as new data is presented), or learn using pre-existing data. This is referred to as batch learning.
- Whether they are instance-based, simply comparing new data to known data, or model-based, involving the detection of patterns and building a predictive model.

These approaches are not mutually exclusive and most algorithms are a combination of the approaches. For example, a typical way to build a spam detector is using an online, model-based supervised learning algorithm.

Learning tasks

There are several distinct types of learning tasks that are partially defined by the type of data that they work on. Based on this, we can divide learning tasks into two broad categories:

- **Unsupervised learning**: Data is unlabeled so the algorithm must infer a relationship between variables or by finding clusters of similar variables
- **Supervised learning**: Uses a labeled dataset to build an inferred function that can be used to predict the label of an unlabeled sample

Whether the data is labeled or not has a predetermining effect on the way a learning algorithm is built.

Unsupervised learning

One of the main drawbacks to supervised learning is that it requires data that is accurately labeled. Most real-world data consists of unlabeled and unstructured data and this is the major challenge to machine learning and the broader endeavor of artificial intelligence. Unsupervised learning plays an important role in finding structure in unstructured data. The division between supervised and unsupervised learning is not absolute. Many unsupervised algorithms are used to together with supervised learning; for example, where data is only partially labeled or when we are trying to find the most important features of a deep learning model.

Clustering

This is the most straightforward unsupervised method. In many cases, it does not matter that the data is unlabeled; what we are interested in is the fact that the data clusters around certain points. Recommender systems that, say, recommend movies or books from an online store often use clustering techniques. An approach here is for an algorithm to analyze a customer's purchase history, comparing it to other customers, and making recommendations based on similarities. The algorithm *clusters* customers' usage patterns into groups. At no time does the algorithm know what the groups are; it is able to work this out for itself. One of the most used clustering algorithms is **k-means**. This algorithm works by establishing cluster centers based on the mean of the observed samples.

Principle component analysis

Another unsupervised method, often used in conjunction with supervised learning, is **principle component analysis** (**PCA**). This is used when we have a large amount of features that may be correlated and we are unsure of the impact each feature has in determining a result. For example, in weather prediction, we could use each meteorological observation as a feature and feed them directly to a model. This means the model would have to analyze a large amount of data, much of it irrelevant. Further, the data may be correlated so that we need to consider not just individual features but how these features interact with each other. What we need is a tool that will reduce this large amount of possibly correlated and redundant features into a small number of principle components. PCA belongs to a type of algorithm called **dimensionality reduction** because this reduces the number of dimensions in the input dataset.

Reinforcement learning

Reinforcement learning is somewhat different to other methods and is often classified as an unsupervised method because the data it uses is not labeled in the supervised sense. Reinforcement learning probably comes closer to the way humans interact and learn from the world than other methods. In reinforcement learning, the learning system is called an **agent** and this agent interacts with an **environment** by observation and by performing **actions.** Each action results in either a **reward** or a **penalty**. The agent must develop a strategy or **policy** to maximize reward and minimize penalties over time. Reinforcement learning has applications in many domains, such as game theory and robotics where the algorithm must learn its environment without direct human prompting.

Supervised learning

In supervised learning, a machine learning model is trained on a labeled dataset. Most successful deep learning models so far have been focused on supervised learning tasks. With supervised learning, each data instance (say, an image or an email), comes with two elements: a set of features, usually denoted as an uppercase X, and a label, denoted with a lower case, y. Sometimes, the label is called the target or answer.

Supervised learning is usually conducted in two stages: a training phase when the model learns the characteristics of the data, and a testing phase, where predictions are made on unlabeled data. It is important that the model is trained and tested on separate datasets, since the goal is to generalize to new data and not precisely learn the characteristics of a single dataset. This can lead to the common problems of over **overfitting** the training set, and consequently underfitting a test set of data.

Classification

Classification is probably the most common supervised machine learning task. There are several types of classification problems based the number of input and output labels. The task of a classification model is to find a pattern in the input features and associate this pattern with a label. A model should learn the distinguishing features of the data and then be able to predict the label of an unlabeled sample. The model essentially builds an inferred function from the training data. We will look at how this function is built shortly. We can distinguish three types of classification models:

- **Binary classification**: As in our toy—no toy example, this involves distinguishing between two labels.

- **Multi-label classification**: Involves distinguishing between more than two classes. For example, if the toy example was extended to distinguish between the types of toy in the image (car, truck, plane, and so on). A common way to solve multi-label classification problems is to divide the problem into multiple binary problems.
- **Multiple output classification**: Each sample may have more than one output label. For example, perhaps the task is to analyze images of scenes and determine what type of toys are in them. Each image can have multiple types of toys and therefore has multiple labels.

Evaluating classifiers

You may think that the best way to measure the performance of a classifier is to count the proportion of successful predictions compared with the total predictions made. However, consider a classification task on a dataset of handwritten digits, where the target is all the digits that are *not* 7. Just guessing that every sample is not 7 will give a success rate, assuming the data is evenly distributed, of 90%. When evaluating classifiers, we must consider four variables:

- **TP true positive**: The predictions that correctly identify a target
- **TN true negative**: The predictions that correctly identify a non-target
- **FP false positive**: Predictions that incorrectly identify a target
- **FN false negative**: Predictions that incorrectly identify a non-target

Two metrics, *precision* and *recall*, are commonly used together to measure the performance of a classifier. *Precision* is defined by the following equation:

$$precision = \frac{TP}{TP + FP}$$

Recall is defined by the following equation:

$$recall = \frac{TP}{TP + FN}$$

We can combine these ideas in what is known as a confusion matrix. It is called confusion matrix, not because it is confusing to understand, but because it tabulates instances where the classifier confuses targets. The following diagram should make this clearer:

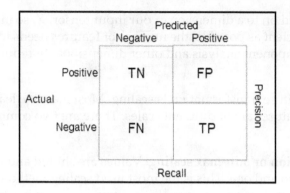

Which measure we use, or give more weight in determining the success or not of a classifier, really depends on the application. There is a trade-off between precision and recall. Improving precision will often result in a reduction in recall. For example, increasing the number of true positives will often mean that the false positive rate is increased. The right balance of precision and recall depends on the requirements of the application. For example, in a medical test for cancer, we probably need higher precision, since a false negative means an instance of cancer remains undiagnosed, with potentially fatal consequences.

Features

It is important to remember that an image detection model does not see an image but a set of pixel color values, or, in the case of a spam filter, a collection of characters in an email. These are raw features of the model. An important part of machine learning is feature transformation. A feature transformation we have already discussed is dimensionality reduction in regard to principle component analysis. The following is a list common feature transformations:

- Dimensionality reduction to reduce the number of features using techniques such as PCA
- Scaling or normalizing features to be within a particular numerical range
- Transforming the feature data type (for example, assigning categories to numbers)
- Adding random or generated data to augment features

Each feature is encoded on to a dimension of our input tensor, X, so in order to make a learning model as efficient as possible, the number of features needs to be minimised. This is where principle component analysis and other dimensionality reduction techniques come in to play.

Another important feature transformation is scaling. Most machine learning models do not perform well when features are of different scales. There are two common techniques used for feature scaling:

- **Normalization or min-max scaling**: Values are shifted and re-scaled to be between zero and one. This is the most used scaling method for neural networks.
- **Standardization**: Subtracts the mean and divides by the variance. This does not bound variables to a particular range, but the resultant distribution has unit variance.

Handling text and categories

What do we do when a feature is a set of categories rather than a number? Suppose we are building a model to predict house prices. A feature of this model could be the cladding material of the house, with possible values such as timber, iron, and cement. How can we encode this feature to be of use to a deep learning model? The obvious solution is to simply assign a real number to each category: say, 1 for timber, 2 for iron, and 3 for cement. The problem with this representation is that it infers that the category values are ordered. That is, timber and iron are somehow closer than timber and cement.

A solution that avoids this is **one-hot encoding**. The feature values are encoded as binary vectors, as shown in the following table:

Timber	1	0	0
Iron	0	1	0
Cement	0	0	1

This solution works well when the number of category values is small. If, for example, the data is a corpus of text, and our task is natural language processing, using one-hot encoding is not practical. The number of category values, and therefore the length of the feature vector, is the number of words in the vocabulary. In this case, the feature vector becomes large and unmanageable.

One-hot encoding uses what is called a sparse representation. Most of the values are 0. As well as not scaling very well, one-hot encoding has another serious drawback for natural language processing. It does not encode a word's meaning, or its relationship to other words. An approach we can use is called dense word embedding. Each word in a vocabulary is represented by a real numbered vector, representing a score for a particular attribute. The general idea is that this vector encodes semantic information relevant to the task at hand. For example, if the task is to analyze movie reviews and determine the genre of the movie based on a review, we could create word embedding, as shown in the following table:

Word	Drama	Comedy	Documentary
Funny	-4	4.5	0
Action	3.5	2.5	2
Suspense	4.5	1.5	3

Here, the leftmost column lists words that may be present in a movie review. Each word is given a score relative to how often it appears in a review of the respective genre. We could build such a table from a supervised learning task that analyzes movie reviews in conjunction with their labeled genre. This trained model could then be applied to non-labeled reviews to determine the most likely genre.

Models

Choosing a model representation is an important task in machine learning. So far, we have been referring to models as black boxes. Some data is put in, and, based on training, the model makes a prediction. Before we look inside this black box, let's review some of the linear algebra that we will need to understand deep learning models.

Linear algebra review

Linear algebra is concerned with the representation of linear equations through the use of matrices. In the algebra taught in high school, we were concerned with scalar, that is, single number, values. We have equations, and rules for manipulating these equations, so that they can be evaluated. The same is true when, instead of scalar values, we use matrices. Let's review some of the concepts involved.

A matrix is simply a rectangular array of numbers. We saw that we added two matrices simply by adding each corresponding element. A matrix can be multiplied by a scalar by simply multiplying every element in the array by the scalar, as shown in the following example:

$$A + B = \begin{bmatrix} a_{00} & a_{01} \\ a_{10} & a_{11} \\ a_{20} & a_{21} \end{bmatrix} + \begin{bmatrix} b_{00} & b_{01} \\ b_{10} & b_{11} \\ b_{20} & b_{21} \end{bmatrix} = \begin{bmatrix} a_{00} + b_{00} & a_{01} + b_{01} \\ a_{10} + b_{10} & a_{11} + b_{11} \\ a_{20} + b_{20} & a_{21} + b_{21} \end{bmatrix}$$

This is an example of matrix addition and, as you would expect, you can perform matrix subtraction in the same way, except of course, rather than add corresponding elements, you subtract them. Note that we can only add or subtract matrices of the same size.

Another common matrix operation is multiplication by a scalar:

$$2 \times \begin{bmatrix} a_{00} & a_{01} \\ a_{10} & a_{11} \\ a_{20} & a_{21} \end{bmatrix} = \begin{bmatrix} 2a_{00} & 2a_{01} \\ 2a_{10} & 2a_{11} \\ 2a_{20} & 2a_{21} \end{bmatrix}$$

Notice the indexing style we use: X_{ij}, where i refers to the row and j refers to the column. There are two conventions when it comes to indexing. Here, I am using zero indexing; that is, indexing starts at zero. This is to keep it consistent with the way we index tensors in PyTorch. Be aware that in some mathematical texts, and depending on what programming language you use, indexing may start at 1. Also, we refer to the size, or the dimension of a matrix, as m by n, where m is the number of rows and n is the number of columns. For example, A and B are both 3 x 2 matrices.

There is a special case of a matrix called a vector. This is simply a n by 1 matrix, so it has one column and any number of rows, as shown in the following example:

$$\begin{bmatrix} a_1 \\ a_2 \\ \cdot \\ \cdot \\ a_n \end{bmatrix}$$

Let's now look at how to multiply a vector with a matrix. In the following example, we multiply a 3 x 2 matrix with a vector of size 2:

$$\begin{bmatrix} a_{00} & a_{01} \\ a_{10} & a_{11} \\ a_{20} & a_{21} \end{bmatrix} \times \begin{bmatrix} b_0 \\ b_1 \end{bmatrix} = \begin{bmatrix} a_{00} \times b_0 + a_{01} \times b_1 \\ a_{10} \times b_0 + a_{11} \times b_1 \\ a_{20} \times b_0 + a_{21} \times b_1 \end{bmatrix}$$

A concrete example may make this clearer:

$$\begin{bmatrix} 1 & 2 \\ 3 & 4 \\ 5 & 6 \end{bmatrix} \times \begin{bmatrix} 7 \\ 8 \end{bmatrix} = \begin{bmatrix} 23 \\ 53 \\ 83 \end{bmatrix}$$

Note that here, the 3 x 2 matrix results in a 3 vector and, in general, an *m* row matrix multiplied by a vector will result in an *m*-sized vector.

We can also multiply matrices with other matrices by combining matrix vector multiplication, as shown in the following example:

$$A \times B = \begin{bmatrix} a_{00} & a_{01} & a_{02} \\ a_{10} & a_{11} & a_{12} \end{bmatrix} \times \begin{bmatrix} b_{00} & b_{01} \\ b_{10} & b_{11} \\ b_{20} & b_{21} \end{bmatrix} = \begin{bmatrix} c_{00} & c_{01} \\ c_{10} & c_{11} \end{bmatrix}$$

Here:

$$c_{00} = a_{00} \times b_{00} + a_{01} \times b_{10} + a_{02} \times b_{20}$$

$$c_{10} = a_{10} \times b_{00} + a_{11} \times b_{01} + a_{12} \times b_{20}$$

$$c_{01} = a_{00} \times b_{01} + a_{01} \times b_{11} + a_{02} \times b_{21}$$

$$c_{11} = a_{10} \times b_{01} + a_{11} \times b_{11} + a_{12} \times b_{21}$$

Another way of understanding this is that we obtain the first column of matrix C by multiplying matrix A with a vector comprising of the first column of matrix B. We obtain the second column of matrix C by multiplying matrix A with a vector obtained from the second column of matrix B.

Let's look at a concrete example:

$$\begin{bmatrix} 3 & 5 & 2 \\ 4 & 3 & 1 \end{bmatrix} \times \begin{bmatrix} 1 & 4 \\ 1 & 2 \\ 5 & 3 \end{bmatrix} = \begin{bmatrix} 18 & 28 \\ 12 & 25 \end{bmatrix}$$

It is important to understand that we can only multiply two matrices if the number of rows in A is equal to the number of columns in B. The resultant matrix will always have the same number of rows as A and the same number of columns as B. Note that matrix multiplication is not commutative; as in the following:

$$A \times B \neq B \times A$$

Matrix multiplication is, however, associative, as shown in the following example:

$$A \times B \times C = (A \times B) \times C = A \times (B \times C)$$

Matrices are useful because we can represent a large number of operations with relatively simple equations. There are two matrix operations that are particularly important for machine learning:

- Transpose
- Inverse

To transpose a matrix, we simply swap the columns and rows, as shown in the following example:

$$A^T = \begin{bmatrix} 1 & 2 \\ 3 & 4 \\ 5 & 6 \end{bmatrix}^T = \begin{bmatrix} 1 & 3 & 5 \\ 2 & 4 & 6 \end{bmatrix}$$

Finding the inverse of a matrix is a little more complicated. In the set of real numbers, the numbers 1 plays the role of **identity**. That is to say, the number 1 multiplied by any other number that equals that number. Also, almost every number has an inverse; that is, a number that when it is multiplied by itself equals 1. For example, the inverse of 2 is 0.5 because two times 0.5 equals 1. It turns out an equivalent idea holds for matrices and tensors. The identity matrix consists of 1s along its primary diagonal and zeros everywhere else, as shown in the following 3 x 3 example:

$$\begin{pmatrix} 1 & 0 & 0 \\ 0 & 1 & 0 \\ 0 & 0 & 1 \end{pmatrix}$$

The identity matrix is the result when we multiply a matrix that is inverse. We write this in the following way:

$$A \times A^{-1} = I$$

Importantly, we can only find the inverse of a square matrix. It is not expected to calculate inverse matrices, or indeed any matrix operation, by hand. That is what computers are good at. Inverting matrices is a non-trivial operation and they are, even for a computer, computationally expensive.

Linear models

The simplest models we will encounter in machine learning are linear models. Solving linear models is important in many different settings, and they form the building blocks of many nonlinear techniques. With a linear model, we attempt to fit training data to a linear function, sometimes called the **hypothesis function**. This is done through a process called linear regression.

The hypothesis function for single variable linear regression has the following form:

$$h(x) = \theta_0 + \theta_1 x$$

Here, θ_0 and θ_1 are the model **parameters** and x is the single independent variable. For our house price example, x could represent the size of floor space and $h(x)$ could represent the predicted house price.

For simplicity, we will begin by looking at just the single variable, or single feature case.

In the following diagram, we show a number of points, representing training data, and an attempt to fit a straight line to these points:

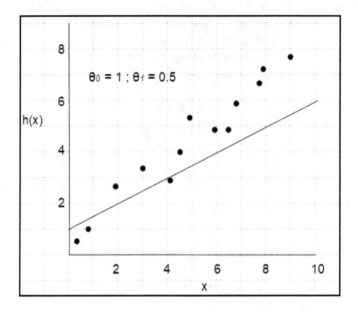

Here, x is the single feature and θ_0 and θ_1 represent the intercept and the slope of the hypothesis function, respectively. Our aim is to find values for θ_0 and θ_1, the model parameters, which will give us our line of best fit in the preceding diagram. In this diagram, θ_0 is set to **1** and θ_1 is set to **0.5**. Therefore, its intercept is **1** and the line has a slope of **0.5**. We can see that most of the training points lie above the line and a few lower-valued points lie below the line. We could guess that θ_1 is probably slightly too low, since the training points appear to have a slightly steeper slope. Also, θ_0 is too high, since there are two data points below the line on the left and the intercept appears to be slightly lower than 1.

It is clear that we need a formal approach to finding the error in the hypothesis function. This is done through what is known as a **cost function**. The cost function measures the total error between the values given by the hypotheses function and the actual values in the data. Essentially, the loss function sums each point's distance from the hypothesis. The cost function is sometimes called the **mean squared error** (**MSE**). This is expressed by the following equation:

$$J_{(\theta_1,\theta_2)} = \frac{1}{2m} \sum_{i=1}^{m} (h_\theta(x^i) - y^i)^2$$

Here, $h_\theta(x^i)$ is the value calculated by the hypothesis for the *i*th training sample, and y^i is its actual value. The difference is squared as statistical convenience, since it ensures the result is always positive. Squaring also adds more weight to larger differences; that is, it places greater importance on outliers. This sum is then divided by *m*, the number of training samples, to calculate the mean. Here, the sum is also divided by two to make subsequent math a little more straightforward.

The final part is to adjust the parameter values so that the hypothesis function fits the training data as closely as possible. We need to find parameter values that minimize the error.

There are two ways we can do this:

- Using gradient descent to iterate over the training set and adjust parameters to minimize a cost function
- Directly computing model parameters, using a *closed-form* equation

Gradient descent

Gradient descent is a general-purpose optimization algorithm that has a wide variety of applications. Gradient descent minimizes the cost function by iteratively adjusting the model parameters. Gradient descent works by taking the partial derivative of the cost function. If we plot the cost function against a parameter value, it forms a convex function, as shown in the following diagram:

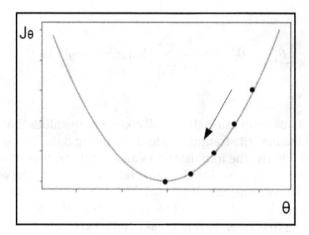

You can see that as we vary θ, from right to left in the preceding diagram, the cost, J_θ, decreases to a minimum and then rises. The aim is that on each iteration of gradient descent, the cost moves closer to the minimum, and then stops once it reaches this minimum. This is achieved using the following update rule:

$$\theta_j := \theta_j - \alpha \frac{\partial}{\partial \theta_j} J(\theta_0 \theta_1)$$

Here, α is the **learning rate,** a settable **hyperparameter**. It is called a hyperparameter to distinguish it from the model parameters, theta. The partial derivative term is the slope of the cost function and this needs to be calculated for both theta *0* and theta *1*. You can see that when the derivative, and therefore the slope, is positive, a positive value is subtracted from the previous value of theta, moving from right to left in the preceding diagram. Alternatively, if the slope is negative, theta increases, moving from right to left. Also, at the minimum, the slope is zero, so gradient descent will stop. This is exactly what we want, since no matter where we start gradient descent, the update rule is guaranteed to move theta toward the minimum.

Substituting the cost function into the preceding equation and then taking the derivative for both values of theta results in the following two update rules, results in the following equations:

$$\theta_0 := \theta_0 - \alpha \frac{1}{m} \sum_{i=1}^{m} (h_\theta(x^{(i)}) - y^{(i)})$$

$$\theta_1 := \theta_1 - \alpha \frac{1}{m} \sum_{i=1}^{m} (h_\theta(x^{(i)}) - y^{(i)}) x^{(i)}$$

On iteration and subsequent updates, theta will converge to values that minimize the cost function, resulting in the best fit straight line to the training data. There are two things that need to be considered. Firstly, the initialization values of theta; that is, where we start gradient descent. In most cases, random initialization works best. The other thing we need to consider is setting the learning rate, alpha (α). This is a number between zero and one. If the learning rate is set too high, then it will likely overshoot the minima. If it is set too low, then it will take too long to converge. It may take some experimentation with the particular model being used; in deep learning, an adaptive learning rate is often used for best results. This is where the learning rate changes, usually getting smaller, on each iteration of gradient descent.

The type of gradient descent we have discussed so far is called **batch gradient descent (BGD)**. This refers to the fact that on each update, the entire training set is used. This means that as the training set gets large, batch gradient descent becomes increasingly slow. On the other hand, batch gradient descent scales much better when there are a large number of features, so it is most often used when there is a smaller training set with a large number of features.

An alternative to batch gradient descent is **stochastic gradient descent (SGD)**. Instead of calculating the gradient using the entire training set, SGD calculates the gradient using a single sample chosen randomly on each iteration. The advantage of SGD is that the entire training set does not have to reside in memory, since on each iteration it works with one instance only. Because stochastic gradient descent chooses samples at random, its behavior is a little less regular than BGD. With batch gradient descent, every iteration smoothly moves the error (J_θ) toward the minima. With SGD, every iteration does not necessarily move the cost closer to the minima. It tends to jump around a bit, moving toward the minima only on average over a number of iterations. This means that it may jump around close to the minima but never actually reach it by the time it completes its iterations. The random nature of SGD can be used to advantage when there is more than one minima, since it may be able to jump out of this local minima and find the global minima. For example, consider the following cost function:

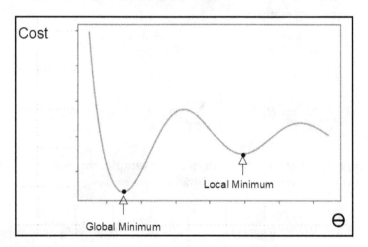

If batch gradient descent were to begin to the right of the **Local Minimum**, it would not be able to find the **Global Minimum**. Fortunately, the cost function for linear regression is always going to be a convex function with a single minima. However, this is not always the case, particularly with neural networks, where the cost function can have a number of local minima.

Multiple features

In a realistic example, we would have more than one feature and each feature has an associated parameter value that requires fitting. We write the hypothesis function for multiple features as follows:

$$h_\theta(x) = \theta_0 x_0 + \theta_1 x_1, \theta_2 x_2, \ldots \theta_n x_n = \theta^T x$$

Here, x_0 is called the bias variable and is set to one, x_1 to x_n are the feature values, and n is the total number of features. Notice that we can write a vectorized version of the hypothesis function. Here, θ is the **parameter vector** and x is the **feature vector.**

The cost function is still basically the same as the single feature case; we are just summing the error. We do, however, need to adjust the gradient descent rules and be clear about the required notation. In the update rules for gradient descent for a single feature, we used the notation for parameter values θ_0 and θ_1. For the multiple feature version, we simply wrap these parameters' values and their associated features into vectors. The parameter vector is notated as θ_j, where the subscript j refers to the feature and is an integer between 1 and n, where n is the number of features.

There needs to be a separate update rule for each parameter. We can generalize these rules as follows:

$$\theta_j := \theta_j - \alpha \frac{1}{m} \sum_{i=1}^{m} (h_\theta(x^{(i)}) - y^{(i)}) x_j^{(i)}$$

There is an update rule for each parameter; so, for example, the update rule for the parameter for feature $j = 1$ would be the following:

$$\theta_1 := \theta_1 - \alpha \frac{1}{m} \sum_{i=1}^{m} (h_\theta(x^{(i)}) - y^{(i)}) x_1^{(i)}$$

 The variables $x^{(i)}$ and $y^{(i)}$ refer, as in the single feature example, to the predicted value and actual value of the ith training sample, respectively. In the multiple feature case, however, instead of being single values, they are now vectors. The value $x_j^{(i)}$ refers to feature j of training sample i, and m is the total number of samples in the training set.

The normal equation

For some linear regression problems, the closed form solution, also known as the **normal equation**, is a better way to find optimum values of theta. If you know calculus, then to minimize the cost function, you can find the partial derivatives of the cost function, with respect to each value of theta, and set each derivative to zero and then solve for each value of theta. Don't worry if you are not familiar with calculus; it turns out that we can derive the normal equation from these partial derivatives and this results in the following equation:

$$mse_{min} = \theta(j) = (X^T \cdot X)^{-1} \cdot X^T \cdot y$$

You may wonder why we need to bother with gradient descent and the added complications this entails, since the normal equation allows us to compute the parameters in one step. The reason is that the computational effort required to invert a matrix is not insignificant. When a feature matrix X becomes large (and remember X is a matrix holding all the values of features for every training sample), then finding the inverse of this matrix simply takes too long. Even though gradient descent involves many iterations, it is still faster than the normal equation for large datasets.

An advantage of the normal equation is that, unlike gradient descent, it does not expect features to be of the same scale. Another advantage of the normal equation is that is not necessary to choose a learning rate.

Logistic regression

We can use the linear regression model to perform binary classification by finding a decision boundary that divides two predicted classes. A common way to do this is by using a `sigmoid` function, defined as the following:

$$g(z) = \frac{1}{1 - e^{-z}}$$

The plot of the `sigmoid` function looks like this:

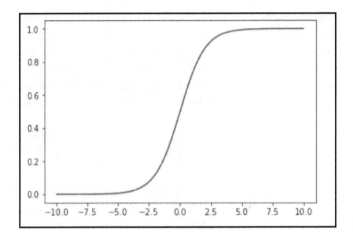

The `sigmoid` function can be used in the hypothesis function, to output a probability, as follows:

$$h_\theta(x) = g(\theta^T x) = P(y = 1 | x : \theta)$$

Here, the output of the hypothesis function is the probability *y = 1* given *x* parameterized by theta. To decide when to predict *y = 0* or *y = 1*, we can use the following two rules:

$$predict \; y = 1 \; if \; h_\theta(x) \geq 0.5$$

$$predict \; y = 0 \; if \; h_\theta(x) < 0.5$$

The characteristics of the `sigmoid` function (that is, having asymptotes at *0* and *1*, and having a value of *0.5* at *z = 0*), has some attractive properties for use with logistic regression problems. Notice that the decision boundary is a property of the parameters of the model, not the training set. We still need to fit the parameters so that the cost, or the error, is minimized. To do this, we need to formalize what we know already.

We have a training set with *m* samples, written as the following equation:

$$\{(x^{(1)}, y^{(1)}), (x^{(2)}, y^{(2)}), \dots, \{(x^{(m)}, y^{(m)})\}$$

Each training sample consists of vector x, of size n, where n is the number of features:

$$X = \begin{bmatrix} x_0 \\ x_1 \\ \cdot \cdot \\ x_n \end{bmatrix} \quad x_0 = 1$$

Each training sample also consists of a value y and, for logistic regression, this value is either zero or one. We also have a hypothesis function for logistic regression, which we can rewrite as the following equation:

$$h_\theta(x) = \frac{1}{1 + e^{-\theta^T x}}$$

Using the same cost function for linear regression, with the hypotheses for logistic regression, we introduce a nonlinearity via the `sigmoid` function. This means that the cost function is no longer convex, and as a result, it may have a number of local minima, which can be a problem for gradient descent. It turns out that a function that works well for logistic regression, and results in a convex cost function, is the following:

$$Cost(h_\theta(x), y) = \{ \begin{matrix} -log(h_\theta(x)) & if & y=1 \\ -log(1-h_\theta(x)) & if & y=0 \end{matrix} \}$$

We can plot these functions for the two cases:

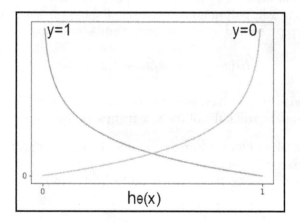

It can be seen from the previous diagrams that, when the label **y** equals **1** and the hypothesis predicts **0**, the cost approaches infinity. Also, when the actual value of **y** is **0**, and the hypothesis predicts **1**, similarly, the cost rises toward infinity. Alternatively, when the hypothesis predicts the correct value, either **0** or **1**, the cost falls to **0**. This is exactly what we want for logistic regression.

Now we need to apply gradient descent to minimize the cost. We can rewrite the logistic regression cost function for binary classification to a more compact form, summing it over multiple training samples, using the following equation:

$$J(\theta) = -\frac{1}{m} [\sum_{m}^{i=1} y^{(i)} \log h_\theta(x^{(i)}) + (1 - y^{(i)} \log(1 - h_\theta(x^{(i)}))]$$

Finally, we can update the parameter values with this update rule:

$$\theta_j := \theta_j - \alpha \frac{1}{m} \sum_{i=1}^{m} (h_\theta(x^{(i)}) - y^{(i)}) x_j^{(i)}$$

Superficially, this looks identical to the update rule for linear regression; however, the hypothesis is a function of the `sigmoid` function, so it actually behaves quite differently.

Nonlinear models

We have seen that linear models, by themselves, fail to represent nonlinear real-world data. A possible solution is to add polynomial features to the hypotheses function. For example, a cubic model can be represented by the following equation:

$$h_\theta(x) = \theta_0 + \theta_1 x^2 + \theta_2 x^2 + \theta_3 x^3$$

Here, we need to choose two derived features to add to our model. These added terms could simply be the square and cube of the size feature in the housing example.

An important consideration when adding polynomial terms is feature scaling. The squared and cubic terms in this model will be of quite different scales. In order for gradient descent to work correctly, it is necessary to scale these added polynomial terms.

Choosing polynomial terms is a way to inject knowledge into a model. For example, simply knowing that house prices tend to flatten out relative to floor space, as the floor space gets large, suggests adding squared and cubic terms, giving us the shape that we expect the data to take. However, feature selection where, say in logistic regression, when we are trying to predict a complicated multidimensional decision boundary, it may mean thousands of polynomial terms. Under such circumstances, the machinery of linear regression grinds to a halt. We will see that neural networks offer a more automated and powerful solution to complicated nonlinear problems.

Artificial neural networks

As the name suggests, ANNs are inspired by their biological counterpart, although the reason is, perhaps, misunderstood. An artificial neuron, or what we will call a **unit**, is grossly simplified compared to a biological neuron, both in terms of functionality and structure. The biological inspiration comes more from the insight that each neuron in a brain performs an identical function regardless of whether it is processing sound, vision, or pondering complex mathematics problems. This single algorithm approach is, fundamentally, the inspiration for ANNs.

An artificial neuron, a unit, performs a single simple function. It adds up its inputs and, dependent on an activation function, gives an output. One of the major benefits of ANNs is that they are highly scalable. Since they are composed of fundamental units, simply adding more units in the right configuration allows ANNs to easily scale to massive, complex data.

The theory of ANNs has been around for quite some time, first proposed in the early 1940's. However, it is not until recently that they have been able to outperform more traditional machine learning techniques. There are three broad reasons for this:

- The improvement in algorithms, notably the implementation of **backpropagation**, allowing an ANN to distribute the error at the output to input layers and adjust activation weights accordingly
- The availability of massive datasets to train ANNs
- The increase in processing power, allowing large-scale ANNs

The perceptron

One of the most simple ANN models is the perceptron, consisting of a single logistic unit. We can represent the perceptron in the following diagram:

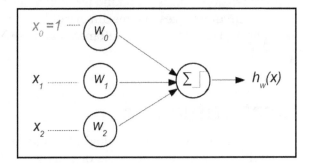

Each of the inputs are associated with a weight and these are fed into the logistic unit. Note that we add a bias feature, $x_0 = 1$. This logistic unit consists of two elements: a function to sum inputs and an activation function. If we use the `sigmoid` as the activation function, then we can write the following equation:

$$h_w(x) = g(x_0 w_0 + x_1 w_1 + x_2 w_2) = g(W^T x) = \frac{1}{1 + e^{-W^T x}}$$

Note that this is exactly the hypothesis we used for logistic regression; we have simply swapped θ for w, to denote to the weights in the logistic unit. These weights are exactly equivalent to the parameters of the logistic regression model.

To create a neural network, we connect these logistic units into layers. The following diagram represents a three-layered neural network. Note that for the sake of clarity, we omit the bias unit:

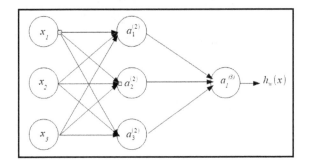

This simple ANN consists of an input layer with three units; one hidden layer, also with three units; and finally, a single unit in the output. We use the notation *ai(j)* to refer to the activation of unit *i* in layer *j* and with $W^{(j)}$ denoting the matrix of weights that map layer *j* to layer *j+1*. Using this notation, we can express the activation of the three hidden units with the following equations:

$$a_1^{(2)} = g(W_{10}^{(1)} x_0 + W_{11}^{(1)} x_1 + W_{12}^{(1)} x_2 + W_{13}^{(1)} x_3)$$

$$a_2^{(2)} = g(W_{20}^{(1)} x_0 + W_{21}^{(1)} x_1 + W_{22}^{(1)} x_2 + W_{23}^{(1)} x_3)$$

$$a_3^{(2)} = g(W_{30}^{(1)} x_0 + W_{31}^{(1)} x_1 + W_{32}^{(1)} x_2 + W_{33}^{(1)} x_3)$$

The activation of the output unit can then be expressed by the following equation:

$$h_\theta(x) = a_2^{(3)} = g(W_{10}^{(2)} a_0^{(2)} + W_{11}^{(2)} a_1^{(2)} + W_{12}^{(2)} a_2^{(2)} + W_{13}^{(2)} a_3^{(2)})$$

Here, $W^{(1)}$ is a 3 x 4 matrix controlling the function mapping between the input, layer one, and the single hidden layer, layer two. The weight matrix $W^{(2)}$, of size 1 X 4, controls the mapping between the hidden layer and the output layer, H. More generally, a network with s_j units in layer *j* and s_k units in layer *j+1* will have a size of s_k by $(s_j)+1$. For example, for a network that has five input units and three units in the next forward layer, layer two, the associated weight matrix, $W^{(1)}$ will be of size 3 x 6.

Having established a hypotheses function, the next step is to formulate a cost function to measure, and ultimately minimize, the error of the model. For classification, the cost function is almost identical to that used for logistic regression. The important difference is that with neural networks, we can add output units to allow multi-class classification. We can write the cost function for multiple outputs as follows:

$$J(W) = -\frac{1}{m}[\sum_{m}^{i=1} \sum_{k=1}^{K} y_k^{(i)} log(h_w(x^{(i)})_k) + (1 - y_k^{(i)} log(1 - h_w(x^{(i)}))_k)]$$

Here, K is the number of output units representing the number of output classes.

Finally, we need to minimize the cost function, which is done using the backpropagation algorithm. Essentially, what this does is backpropagate the error, the gradient of the cost function, from the output units to the input units. To do this, we need to evaluate partial derivatives. That is, we need to compute the following:

$$\frac{\partial}{\partial W_{ij}^{(l)}} J(W)$$

Here, l is the layer, j is the unit, and i is the sample. In other word, for each unit in each layer, and for every sample, we need to calculate the partial derivative, the gradient, of the cost function with respect to each parameter. For example, consider we have a network with four layers. Consider also that we are working with a single sample. We need to find the error at each layer, beginning at the output. The error at the output is just the error of the hypothesis:

$$\delta_j^{(4)} = a_j^{(4)} - y_j = h_w(x)_j - y_j$$

This is a vector of the error for each unit, j. The superscript *(4)* indicates this is the fourth layer; that is, the output layer. It turns out that, through some complicated math we do not need to worry about here, the error for the two hidden layers can be calculated with the following equations:

$$\delta^{(3)} = (W^{(3)})^T \delta^{(4)} .*(a^{(3)} .*(1 - a^{(3)}))$$

$$\delta^{(2)} = (W^{(2)})^T \delta^{(3)} .*(a^{(2)} .*(1 - a^{(2)}))$$

The .*operator here is element-wise vector multiplication. Notice that the error vector of the next forward layer is required in each of these equations. That is, to calculate the error in layer three, the error vector of the output layer is required. Similarly, to calculate the error in layer two requires the error vector of layer three.

This is how backpropagation works with a single sample. To loop across an entire dataset, we need to accumulate the gradients for each unit and each sample. So, for each sample in the training set, the neural net performs forward propagation to compute the activation for the hidden layers and the output layer. Then, for the same sample, that is within the same loop, the output error can be calculated. Consequently, we are able calculate the error for each previous layer in turn, and the neural net does exactly this, accumulating each gradient in a matrix. The loop begins again performing the identical set of operations on the next sample, and these gradients are also accumulated in the error matrix. We can write an update rule as follows:

$$\triangle_{ij}^l := \triangle_{ij}^l + a_{ij}^{(l)} \delta^{l+1)}$$

The capital delta is the matrix that stores the accumulated gradients by adding the activation for layer l, unit j, and sample i, then multiplying it with the associated error of the next forward layer for this same sample, i. Finally, once we have made a pass over the entire training set—an epoch—we can calculate the derivative of the cost function with respect to each parameter:

$$D_{ij}^{(l)} = \frac{1}{m} \triangle_{ij}^{(l)} = \frac{\partial}{\partial W_{ij}^{(l)}} J(W)$$

Once again, it is not necessary to know the formal proof for this; it's just to give you some intuitive understanding of the mechanics of backpropagation.

Summary

We have covered a lot of material in this chapter. Don't worry if you do not understand some of the mathematics presented here. The aim is to give you some intuition into how some common machine learning algorithms work, not to have a complete understanding of the theory behind these algorithms. After reading this chapter, you should have some understanding of the following:

- General approaches to machine learning, including knowing the difference between supervised and unsupervised methods, online and batch learning, and rule-based, as opposed to model-based, learning
- Some unsupervised methods and their applications, such as clustering and principle component analysis
- Types of classification problems, such as binary, multi-class, and multi-out classification
- Features and feature transformations
- The mechanics of linear regression and gradient descent
- An overview of neural networks and the backpropagation algorithm

In Chapter 3, *Computational Graphs and Linear Models*, we will apply some of these concepts using PyTorch. Specifically, we will show how to find the gradients of functions by building a simple linear model. You will also gain a practical understanding of backpropagation by implementing a simple neural network.

Computational Graphs and Linear Models

By now you should have an understanding of the theory of linear models and neural networks, as well as a knowledge of the fundamentals of PyTorch. In this chapter, we will be putting all this together by implementing some ANNs in PyTorch. We will focus on the implementation of linear models, and show how they can be adapted to perform multi-class classification. We will discuss the following topics in relation to PyTorch:

- autograd
- Computational graphs
- Linear regression
- Logistic regression
- Multi-class classification

autograd

As we saw in the last chapter, much of the computational work for ANNs involves calculating derivatives to find the gradient of the cost function. PyTorch uses the `autograd` package to perform automatic differentiation of operations on PyTorch tensors. To see how this works, let's look at an example:

```
1  import torch
2  a= torch.tensor([[1,2,3],[4,5,6]], requires_grad=True, dtype=torch.float)
3  b= a +2
4  c=2*b*b
5  out=c.mean()
6  out.backward()
7  print(a.grad)

tensor([[ 2.0000,  2.6667,  3.3333],
        [ 4.0000,  4.6667,  5.3333]])
```

In the preceding code, we create a 2 x 3 torch tensor and, importantly, set the `requires_grad` attribute to `True`. This enables the calculation of gradients across subsequent operations. Notice also that we set the `dtype` to `torch.float`, since this is the data type that PyTorch uses for automatic differentiation. We perform a sequence of operations and then take the mean of the result. This returns a tensor containing a single scalar. This is normally what `autograd` requires to calculate the gradient of the preceding operations. This could be any sequence of operations; the important point is that all these operations are recorded. The input tensor, a, is tracking these operations, even though there are two intermediate variables. To see how this works, let's write down the sequence of operations performed in the preceding code with respect to the input tensor a:

$$out = \frac{1}{6} \sum_i 2(a_i + 2)^2$$

Here, the summation and division by six represents taking the mean across the six elements of the tensor a. For each element, a_i, the operations assigned to the tensor b, the addition of two, and c, squaring and multiplying by two, are summed and divided by six.

Calling `backward()` on the *out* tensor calculates the derivative of the previous operation. This derivative can be written as the following, and if you know a little bit of calculus you will be able to easily confirm this:

$$\frac{\partial\ out}{\partial a} = \frac{4(a_i + 2)}{6}$$

When we substitute the values of *a* into the right-hand side of the preceding equation, we do, indeed, get the values contained in the a.grad tensor, printed out in the preceding code.

It is sometimes necessary to perform operations that do not need to be tracked on tensors that have `requires_grad=True`. To save memory and computational effort, it is possible to wrap such operations in a `with torch.no_grad():` block. For example, observe the following code:

```
1  print(a.requires_grad)
2  with torch.no_grad():
3       print((a**2).requires_grad)

True
False
```

To stop PyTorch tracking operations on a tensor, use the `.detach()` method. This prevents future tracking of operations and detaches the tensor from the tracking history:

```
1  print a.detach().requires_grad

False
```

Notice that if we try to calculate gradients a second time, by, for example calling `out.backward()`, we will again generate an error. If we do need to calculate gradients a second time, we need to retain the computational graph. This is done by setting the `retain_graph` parameter to `True`. For example, observe the following code:

```
1  a= torch.ones((2,3), requires_grad=True)
2  b= a +2
3  c=2*b*b
4  out=c.mean()
5  out.backward(retain_graph=True)
6  print a.grad
7  out.backward()
8  print(a.grad)
tensor([[ 2.,  2.,  2.],
        [ 2.,  2.,  2.]])
tensor([[ 4.,  4.,  4.],
        [ 4.,  4.,  4.]])
```

Notice that calling `backward` a second time adds the gradients to the ones already stored in the `a.grad` variable. Note that the `grad` buffer is freed once `backward()` is called without setting the `retain_graph` parameter to `True`.

Computational graphs

To get a better understanding of this, let's look at what precisely a computational graph is. We can draw the graph for the function we have been using so far as follows:

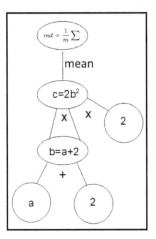

Here, the leaves of the graph represent the inputs and parameters of each layer, and the output represents the loss.

Typically, unless `retain_graph` is set to `True`, on each iteration of an epoch, PyTorch will create a new computational graph.

Linear models

Linear models are an essential way to understand the mechanics of ANNs. Linear regression is used to both predict a continuous variable and also, in the case of logistic regression for classification, to predict a class. Neural networks are extremely useful for multi-class classification, since their architecture can be naturally adapted to multiple inputs and outputs.

Linear regression in PyTorch

Let's see how PyTorch implements a simple linear network. We could use `autograd` and `backward` to manually iterate through gradient descent. This unnecessarily low-level approach encumbers us with a lot of code that will be difficult to maintain, understand, and upgrade. Fortunately, PyTorch has a very straightforward object approach to building ANNs, using classes to represent models. The model classes we customize inherit all the foundation machinery required for building ANNs using the super class, `torch.nn.Module`. The following code demonstrates the standard way to implement modules (in this case, a `linearModel`) in PyTorch:

```
1  import torch
2  import torch.nn as nn
3
4  #Standard model class
5  class LinearModel(nn.Module):
6      def __init__(self, in_dim, out_dim):
7          super(LinearModel, self).__init__()
8          self.linear = nn.Linear(in_dim, out_dim)
9
10      def forward(self,x):
11          out = self.linear(x)
12          return out
13
14  model = LinearModel(1, 1)
```

The nn.`Module` is the base class and is called through the super function on initialization. This ensures that it inherits all the functionality encapsulated in nn.`Module`. We set a variable, `self.Linear`, to the nn.`Linear` class, reflective of the fact we are building a linear model. Remember, a linear function with one independent variable, that is one feature, x, can be written in the following way:

$$y = w_0 + x w_1$$

The nn.`linear` class contains two learnable variables: `bias` and `weight`. In our single feature model, these are the two parameters, w_0 and w_1, respectively. When we train a model, these variables are updated, ideally to values that approach the line of best fit to the data. Finally, in the preceding code, we instantiate the model by creating the variable, `model`, and setting it to our `LinearModel` class.

Before we can run the model, we need set the learning rate, the type of optimizer to use, and the criteria to measure the loss. This is done with the following code:

```
1 learnRate = 0.01
2 optimiser =  torch.optim.SGD(model.parameters(), lr =learnRate)
3 criterion = nn.MSELoss()
```

As you can see, we set the learning rate to 0.01. This tends to be a good starting point; any higher and the optimizer may overshoot the optimum, any lower and it may take too long to find it. We set the `optimiser` to stochastic gradient descent, passing it the items we need it to optimize (in this case, the model parameters), and also the learning rate to use on each step of the gradient descent. Finally, we set the loss criteria; that is, the criteria gradient descent will be used to measure the loss, and here we set it to the mean square error.

To test this linear model, we need to feed it some data and, for testing purposes, we create a simple dataset, x, consisting of numbers from 1 to 10. We create the output, or target, data by applying a linear transformation on the input values. Here, we use the linear function, y= 3*x + 5. This is coded as follows:

```
1 x_train = torch.tensor([1,2,3,4,5,6,7,8,9,10], dtype=torch.float).reshape(-1,1)
2 y_train = torch.tensor([3*x+5 for x in x_train]).reshape(-1,1)
```

Note that we need to reshape these tensors so the input, x, and the target, y, have the same shapes. Note also that we do not need to set `autograd`, as this is all handled by the model class. We do, however, need to tell PyTorch that the input tensor is of data type `torch.float`, since, by default, it will treat the list as integers.

Now we are ready to run the linear model and to do this we run it in a loop for each epoch. This training cycle consists of the following three steps:

1. A forward pass over the training set
2. A backward pass to compute the loss
3. Updating the parameters according to the gradient of the loss function

This is done with the following code:

```
1  epochs = 1000
2  for epoch in range(epochs):
3      epoch +=1
4      inputs = x_train
5      labels = y_train
6      out = model(inputs)
7      optimiser.zero_grad()
8      loss = criterion(out, labels)
9      loss.backward()
10     optimiser.step()
11     predicted = model.forward(x_train)
12     print('epoch{}, loss {}'.format(epoch, loss.item()))
13
```

```
epoch1, loss 564.4509887695312
epoch2, loss 30.568267822265625
epoch3, loss 6.033814907073975
epoch4, loss 4.869321346282959
epoch5, loss 4.777401924133301
```

We set `epoch` to `1000`. Remember, each `epoch` is one full pass over the training set. The model inputs are set to the x values of the dataset; in this case, it is simply the sequence of numbers from 1 to 10. We set the labels to the y values; in this case, the values calculated by our function, `2*x + 5`.

Importantly, we need to clear the gradients so that they do not accumulate over epochs and distort the model. This is achieved by calling the `zero_grad()` function on the optimizer on each epoch. The out tensor is set to the linear models output, calling the forward function of the `LinearModel` class. This model applies a linear function, with the current estimate of the parameters, and gives a predicted output.

Once we have an output, we can calculate the loss using the mean square error, comparing the actual y values to the values calculated by the model. Next, the gradient can calculate by calling `backwards()` on the `loss` function. This determines the next step of the gradient descent, enabling the `step()` function to update parameter values. We also create a `predicted` variable that will store the predicted values of x. We will use this shortly when we plot the predictions and actual values of x.

To understand if our model is working, we print the loss on each epoch. Notice the loss is decreasing each time, indicating it is working as expected. Indeed, by the time the model completes `1000` epochs, the loss is quite small. We can print the model's state (that is, the parameter values) by running the following code:

```
1 print(model.state_dict())
```
```
OrderedDict([('linear.weight', tensor([[ 3.0113]])), ('linear.bias', tensor([ 4.9210]))])
```

Here, the `linear.weight` tensor consists of the single element of value `3.0113` and the `linear.bias` tensor contains the value `4.9210`. This is very close to the values of w_0 (5) and w_1 (3) that we used to create the linear dataset through the y=3x + 5 function.

To make this a little more interesting, let's see what happens when, instead of using a linear function to create the labels, we add a squared term to the function (for example, y= $3x^2$ + 5). We can visualize the result of the model by graphing the predicted values against the actual values. We can see the result with the following code:

```
1 import matplotlib.pyplot as plt
2 x = x_train.detach().numpy()
3 plt.plot x, predicted.detach().numpy(), label = 'predicted'
4 plt.plot(x, y_train.detach().numpy(),'go', label = 'from data')
5 plt.legend()
6 plt.show()
```

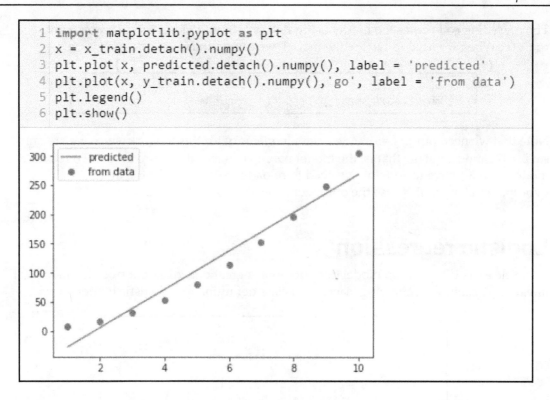

We have used the $y = 3x^2 + 5$ function to generate the labels. The squared term gives the training set the characteristic curve and the linear model's predictions are the best fit straight line. You can see that after 1,000 epochs, this model does a reasonably good job at fitting the curve.

Saving models

Once a model has been built and trained, it is common to want to save the model's state. This is not so important in cases like this, when training takes an insignificant amount of time. However, with large datasets, and many parameters, training can potentially take hours our even days to complete. Clearly, we do not want to retrain a model every time we need it to make a prediction on new data. To save a trained model's parameters, we simply run the following code:

```
1 torch.save(model.state_dict(), 'testmodel.pkl')
```

The preceding code saves the model using Python's inbuilt object serialization module, `pickle`. When we need to restore the model, we can do the following:

```
1  model = LinearModel(1,1)
2  model.load_state_dict(torch.load('testmodel.pkl'))
```

Note that we need our `LinearModel` class in memory for this to work, since we are only saving the model's state; that is, the model parameters, not the entire model. To retrain the model once we have restored it, we need to reload the data and set the model hyperparameters (in this case the optimizer, learning rate, and criterion).

Logistic regression

A simple logistic regression model does not look a great deal different from the model for linear regression. The following is a typical class definition for a logistic model:

```
1  import torch
2  import torch.nn as nn
3  import torch.nn.functional as func
4
5  class LogisticModel(nn.Module):
6      def __init__(self, in_dim, out_dim):
7          super(LogisticModel, self).__init__()
8          self.linear = nn.Linear(in_dim, out_dim)
9
10     def forward(self,x):
11         out = func.sigmoid(self.linear(x))
12         return out
13
14 model = LogisticModel(1, 1)
```

Notice that we still use a linear function when we initialize the `model` class. However, for logistic regression, we need an activation function. Here, this is applied when `forward` is called. As usual, we instantiate the model into our `model` variable.

Next, we set the criterion and optimizer:

```
1  criterion = torch.nn.BCELoss(size_average=True)
2  optimiser =  torch.optim.SGD(model.parameters(), lr =0.01)
```

We still use stochastic gradient descent; however, we need to change the criterion for the loss function.

With linear regression, we used the MSELoss function to calculate the mean square error. For logistic regression, we are working with probabilities represented by values between zero and 1. It does not make much sense to calculate the mean squared error of a probability; instead, a common technique is to use the cross-entropy loss or log loss. Here, we use the BCELoss function, or **binary cross-entropy loss**. The theory behind this is a little involved. What is important to understand is that it is essentially a logarithmic function that better captures the notion of a probability. Because it is logarithmic, as a predicted probability approaches 1, the log loss slowly decreases toward zero given a correct prediction. Remember, we are trying to calculate a penalty for an incorrect prediction. The loss must increase as the prediction diverges from the true value. Cross-entropy loss penalizes predictions that have high confidence (that is, they are close to 1, and are incorrect) and, conversely, rewards predictions that have lower confidence but are correct.

We can train the model with the identical code used for linear regression, running each epoch in a `for` loop where we do a forward pass to calculate an output, a backward pass to calculate the loss gradient, and finally, update the parameters.

Let's make this a little more concrete by creating a practice example. Suppose we are trying to categorize the species of an insect by some numerical measure, say the length of its wings. We have some training data as follows:

```
1 x_train = torch.tensor([[1.6],[2.1],[1.3],[4.8],[3.5]], dtype=torch.float).reshape(-1,1)
2 y_train = torch.tensor([[0],[0],[0],[1],[1]], dtype=torch.float).reshape(-1,1)
```

Here, the x_train values could represent the wing length in millimeters and the y_train values each sample's label; one indicated the sample belongs to the target species. Once we have instantiated the LogisticModel class, we can run it using the standard running code.

Once we have trained the model, we can test it using some new data:

```
1  test=torch.tensor([[0.1], 1.5 ,[2.3],[3.0],[6.4]])
2  results = model(test)
3  for result in results:
4      if result <= 0.5:
5          print(result,'false')
6      else: print(result, 'true')
```

```
tensor([ 0.3011]) false
tensor([ 0.4324]) false
tensor([ 0.5133]) true
tensor([ 0.5837]) true
tensor([ 0.8483]) true
```

Activation functions in PyTorch

Part of the trick that makes ANNs perform as well as they do is the use of nonlinear activation functions. A first thought is simply to use a step function. In this case, an output from a particular occurs only when the input exceeds zero. The problem with the step function is that it cannot be differentiated, since it does not have a defined gradient. It consists only of flat sections and is discontinuous at zero.

Another method is to use a linear activation function; however, this restricts our output to a linear function as well. This is not what we want, since we need to model highly nonlinear real-world data. It turns out that we can inject nonlinearity into our networks by using nonlinear activation functions. The following is a plot for popular activation functions:

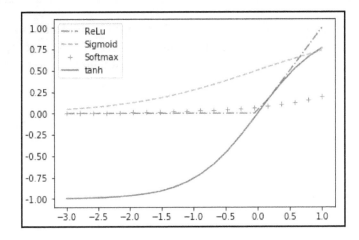

The ReLU, or **rectified linear unit**, is generally considered the most popular activation function. Even though it is non- differentiable at zero, it has a characteristic elbow that can make gradient descent jump around, and it does, in practice, work very well. One of the advantages of the ReLU function is that it is very fast to compute. Also, it does not have a maximum value; it continues to rise to infinity as its input rises. This can be advantageous in certain situations.

We have already met the sigmoid function; its major advantage is that is is differentialable at all input values. This can help in situations where the ReLU function causes erratic behavior during gradient descent. The sigmoid function, unlike ReLU, is constrained by asymptotes. This also can used beneficial for some ANNs.

The softmax function is typically used on output layers for multi-class classification. Remember, multiclass classification, in contrast with multi-label classification, has only one true output. In such cases, we need the predicted target to be as close to 1 as possible and all other outputs close to zero. The softmax function is a nonlinear form of normalization. We need to normalize the output to ensure we are approximating the probability distribution of the input data. Rather than use linear normalization by simply dividing all outputs by their sum, softmax applies a nonlinear exponential function that increases the impact of outlying data points. This tends to increase a network's sensitivity by increasing its reaction to low stimuli. It is computationally more complex than other activation functions; however, it turns out to be an effective generalization of the sigmoid function for multi-class classification.

The tanh activation function, or hyperbolic tangent function, is primarily used for binary classification. It has asmpotopes at −1 and 1 and is often used as an alternative to the sigmoid function, where strongly negative input values cause the sigmoid to output values very close to zero, causing the gradient descent to get stuck. The tanh function will output negatively in such situations, allowing the calculation of meaningful parameters.

Multi-class classification example

So far, we have been using trivial examples to demonstrate core concepts in PyTorch. We are now ready to explore a more real-world example. The dataset we will be using is the MNIST dataset of hand-written digits from 0 to 9. The task is to correctly identify each sample image with the correct digit.

The classification model we will be building consists of several layers and these are outlined in the following diagram:

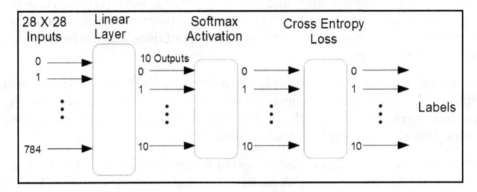

The images we are working with are 28 x 28 pixels in size, and each pixel in each image is characterized by a single number, indicating its gray scale. This is why we need 28 x 28 or 784 inputs to the model. The first layer is a linear layer with 10 outputs, one output for each label. These outputs are fed into to the `softmax` activation layer and cross-entropy loss layer. The 10 output dimensions represent the 10 possible classes, the digits zero to nine. The output with the highest value indicates the predicted label of a given image.

We begin by importing the required libraries, as well as the `MNIST` dataset:

```
1 import torch
2 import torch.nn as nn
3 import torchvision.datasets as dsets
4 import torchvision.transforms as trans
5
6 trainSet = dsets.MNIST(root='./data', train = True, transform=trans.ToTensor(), download=True)
```

Now let's print out some information about the `MNIST` dataset:

```
1 print('Number of images {}'.format(len(trainSet)))
2 print('Type {}'.format(type(trainSet[0][0])))
3 print 'Size of each image {}'.format(trainSet[0][0].size())

Number of images 60000
Type <class 'torch.Tensor'>
Size of each image torch.Size([1, 28, 28])
```

The `len` function returns the number of separate items (in this case, single images) in the dataset. Each one of these images is encoded as a type tensor and the size of each image is 28 x 28 pixels. Each pixel in the image is assigned a single number, indicating its gray scale.

To define our multi-class classification model, we are going to use the exactly the same model definition that we used for linear regression:

```
1 class MultiLogisticModel(nn.Module):
2     def __init__(self, in_dim, out_dim):
3         super(MultiLogisticModel, self).__init__()
4         self.linear = nn.Linear(in_dim, out_dim)
5
6     def forward(self,x):
7         out =self.linear(x)
8         return out
```

Even though, ultimately, we need to perform logistic regression, we achieve the required activation and nonlinearity in a slightly different way to the binary case. You will notice that in the model definition, the output returned by the forward function is simply a linear function. Instead of using the `sigmoid` function, as we did in the previous binary classification example, here we use the `softmax` function, which is assigned with the loss criterion. The following code sets up these variables and instantiates the model:

```
1 in_dim = 28*28 #input dimensions
2 out_dim = 10 #output dimensions
3 model = MultiLogisticModel(in_dim, out_dim) #instantiate model
4 criterion = nn.CrossEntropyLoss()  #instantiate the loss class
5 optimiser = torch.optim.SGD(model.parameters(), lr=.001) #instantiate the optimiser class
```

The `CrossEntropyLoss()` function essentially adds two layers to the network: a `softmax` activation function and a cross-entropy loss function. Each input to the network takes one pixel of the image, so our input dimension is 28 x 28 = 784. The optimizer uses stochastic gradient descent and a learning rate of .0001.

Next, we set a batch size, the number of `epochs` to run the model, and create a data loader object so the model can iterate over the data:

```
1 batchSize = 100
2 epochs = 5
3 trainloader = torch.utils.data.DataLoader dataset=trainSet, batch_size=batchSize, shuffle = True |
```

Setting a batch size feeds the data into the model in specific-sized chunks. Here, we feed the model in batches of `100` images. The number of iterations (that is, the total number of forward-backward traversals of the network), can be calculated by dividing the length of the dataset by the batch size, and multiplying this by the number of `epochs`. In this example, we have 5 x 60,000/100 = 3,000 iterations in total. It turns out this is a much more efficient and effective way to work with moderate to large datasets, since, with finite memory, loading the entire data may not be possible. Also, the model tends to make better predictions since it is trained on a different subsets of data with each batch. Setting `shuffle` to `True` shuffles the data on each `epoch`.

To run this model, we need to create an outer loop that loops through the `epochs` and an inner loop that loops through each batch. This is achieved with the following code:

```
 1  for epoch in range(epochs):
 2
 3      runningLoss = 0.0
 4      for i, (images,labels) in enumerate(trainloader):
 5          images = images.view(-1, 28 * 28)
 6          optimiser.zero_grad()
 7          outputs = model(images)
 8          loss = criterion(outputs, labels)
 9          loss.backward()
10          optimiser.step()
11          runningLoss += loss.item()
12
13      print(runningLoss)

1213.2532706260681
968.1708756685257
809.9442014694214
704.4292406439781
630.6951693296432
```

This is similar to the code we have used to run all our models so far. The only difference here is that the model enumerates over each batch in `trainloader` rather than iterating over the entire dataset at once. Here, we print out the loss on each epoch and, as expected, this loss is decreasing.

We can make a prediction using the model by making a forward pass:

```
1 predicted = model.forward(images)
2 predicted.size()
```

```
torch.Size([100, 10])
```

The size of the predicted variable is 100 by 10. This represents the predictions for the 100 images in the batch. For each image, the model outputs a 10 element prediction tensor, containing a value representing the relative strength of each label at each of its 10 outputs. The following code prints out the first prediction tensor and the actual label:

```
1 print 'predictions {}'.format(predicted[0])
2 print('labels {}'.format(labels[0]))
```

```
predictions tensor([-1.2102,  1.3957, -0.8418, -0.2278, -0.7412, -0.0017, -0.6341,
        0.9142,  0.1112,  0.7837])
labels 1
```

 If we look closely at the previous output, we see that the model correctly predicted the label since the second element, representing the digit 1, contains the highest value of 1.3957. We can see the relative strength of this prediction by comparing it to other values in the tensor. For example, we can see that the next strongest prediction was for the number 7, with a value of 0.9142.

You will see that the model is not correct for every image and to begin to evaluate and improve our models, we need to be able to measure its performance. The most straightforward way is to measure its success rate; that is, the proportion of correct results. To do this, we create the following function:

```
1 import numpy as np
2 def successRate(predicted, labels):
3     predict = [np.argmax(p.detach().numpy()) for p in predicted]
4     actual = [labels[i].item() for i in range(len(predicted))]
5     correct = [i for i, j in zip(predict, actual) if i == j]
6     return(len(correct)/(len(predict)))
```

Here, we use string comprehensions, firstly to create a list of predictions by finding the maximum of each output. Next, we create a list of labels to compare the predictions. We create a list of correct values by comparing each element in the `predict` list with the corresponding element in the `actual` list. Finally, we return the success rate by dividing the number of correct values with the total number of predictions made. We can calculate the success rate of our model by calling this function with the output predictions and the labels:

```
1 successRate(predicted, labels)
```
```
0.83
```

Here, we get a success rate of 83%. Note that this is calculated using images the model has already trained on. To truly test the model's performance, we need to test it on images it has not seen before. We do this with the following code:

```
1 testSet = dsets.MNIST(root='./data', train = False, transform=trans.ToTensor(), download=True)
2 testloader = torch.utils.data.DataLoader(dataset=trainSet, batch_size = 10000, shuffle = True)
3
4 testData = iter(testloader)
5 images, labels = testData.next()
6 output = model(images.view(-1, 28 * 28))
7 successRate(output,labels)
```
```
0.8255
```

Here, we have tested the model using the entire 10,000 images in the MNIST test set. We create an iterator from the data loader object and then load them in to the two tensors, `images` and `labels`. Next, we get an output (here, a 10 by 10,000 prediction tensor), by passing the model test images. Finally, we run the `SuccessRate` function with the output and labels. The value is only slightly lower than the success rate on the training set, so we can be reasonably confident that this is an accurate measure of the model's performance.

Summary

In this chapter, we have explored linear models and applied them to the tasks of linear regression, logistic regression, and multi-class classification. We have seen how autograd calculates gradients and how PyTorch works with computational graphs. The multi-class classification model we built did a reasonable job of predicting hand-written digits; however, its performance is far from optimal. The best deep learning models are able to get near 100% accuracy on this dataset.

We will see in Chapter 4, *Convolutional Networks*, how adding more layers and using convolutional networks can improve performance.

4
Convolutional Networks

Previously, we built several simple networks to solve regression and classification problems. These illustrated the basic code structure and concepts involved in building ANNs with PyTorch.

In this chapter, we will extend simple linear models by adding layers and using convolutional layers to solve nonlinear problems found in real-world examples. Specifically, we will cover the following topics:

- Hyper-parameters and multilayered networks
- Build a simple benchmarking function to train and test models
- Convolutional networks

Hyper-parameters and multilayered networks

Now that you understand the process of building, training, and testing models, you will see that expanding these simple networks to increase performance is relatively straightforward. You will find that nearly all models we build consist, essentially, of the following six steps:

1. Import data and create iterable data-loader objects for the training and test sets
2. Build and instantiate a model class
3. Instantiate a loss class
4. Instantiate an optimizer class
5. Train the model
6. Test the model

Of course, once we complete these steps, we will want to improve our models by adjusting a set of hyper-parameters and repeating the steps. It should be mentioned that although we generally consider hyper-parameters things that are specifically set by a human, the setting of these hyper-parameters can be partially automated, as we shall see in the case of the learning rate. Here are the most common hyper-parameters:

- The learning rate of gradient descent
- The number of epochs to run the model
- The type of nonlinear activation
- The depth of the network, that is, the number of hidden layers
- The width of the network, that is, the number of neurons in each layer
- The connectivity of the network (for example, convolutional networks)

We have already worked with some of these hyper-parameters. We know the learning rate, if set too small, will take more time than necessary to find the optimum, and if set too large, will overshoot and behave erratically. The number of epochs is the number of complete passes over the training set. We would expect that as we increase the number of epochs, the accuracy will improve on each epoch, given limitations on the dataset and the algorithm used. At some point, the accuracy will plateau and training over more epochs is a waste of resources. If the accuracy decreases over the first few epochs, one of the most likely causes is that the learning rate is set too high.

Activation functions play a critical role in classification tasks and the effect of different types of activation can be somewhat subtle. It is generally agreed that the ReLU, or rectified linear function, performs best on the most common practice datasets. This is not to say that other activation functions, particularly the hyperbolic tangent or tanh function and variations on these, such as leaky ReLU, can produce better results under certain conditions.

As we increase the depth, or number of layers, we increase the learning power of the network, enabling it to capture more complex features of the training set. Obviously this increased ability is very much dependant on the size and complexity of the dataset and the task. With small datasets and relatively simple tasks, such as digit classification with MNIST, a very small number of layers (one or two) can give excellent results. Too many layers waste resources and tend to make the network overfit or behave erratically.

Much of this is true when we come to increasing the width, that is, the number of units in each layer. Increasing the width of a linear network is one of the most the most efficient ways to boost learning power. When it comes to convolutional networks, as we will see, not every unit is connected to every unit in the next forward layer; connectivity, that is, the number of input and output channels in each layer, is critical. We will look at convolutional networks shortly, but first we need to develop a framework to test and evaluate our models.

Benchmarking models

Benchmarking and evaluation are core to the success of any deep learning exploration. We will develop some simple code to evaluate two key performance measures: the accuracy and the training time. We will use the following model template:

```python
import torch
import torch.nn as nn
class Model4_1(nn.Module):
    def __init__(self):
        super(Model4_1, self).__init__()
        self.lin1 = nn.Linear(784, 100)
        self.relu = nn.ReLU()
        self.lin2 = nn.Linear(100, 10)

    def forward(self, x):
        out = self.lin1(x)
        out = self.relu(out)
        out = self.lin2(out)
        return out

model4_1 = Model4_1()
```

This model is the most common and basic linear template for solving MNIST. You can see we initialize each layer, in the init method, by creating a class variable that is assigned to a PyTorch nn object. Here, we initialize two linear functions and a ReLU function. The nn.Linear function takes an input size of 28*28 or 784. This is the size of each of the training images. The output channels or the width of the network are set to 100. This can be set to anything, and in general a higher number will give better performance within the constraints of computing resources and the tendency for wider networks to overfit training data.

In the `forward` method, we create an `out` variable. You can see that the out variable is passed through an ordered sequence consisting of a linear function, a ReLU function, and another linear function before being returned. This is a fairly typical network architecture, consisting of alternating linear and nonlinear layers.

Let's now create two more models, replacing the ReLU function with the tanh and sigmoid activation functions. Here is the tanh version:

```
1  class Model4_2(nn.Module):
2      def __init__(self):
3          super(Model4_2, self).__init__()
4          self.lin1 = nn.Linear(784, 100)
5          self.tanh = nn.Tanh()
6          self.lin2 = nn.Linear(100, 10)
7
8      def forward(self, x):
9          out = self.lin1(x)
10         out = self.tanh(out)
11         out = self.lin2(out)
12         return out
13
14 model4_2 = Model4_2()
```

You can see we simply changed the name and replaced the `nn.RelU()` function with `nn.Tanh()`. Create a third model in exactly the same way, replacing `nn.Tanh()` with `nn.Sigmoid()`. Don't forget to change the name in the super constructor and in the variable used to instantiate the model. Also remember to change the forward function accordingly.

Now, let's create a simple `benchmark` function that we can use to run and record the accuracy and training time of each of these models:

```
 1 import torch.optim as optim
 2 import time
 3
 4 def benchmark(trainLoader, model, epochs=1, lr=0.01):
 5     model.__init__()
 6     start=time.time()
 7     optimiser = optim.SGD(model.parameters(), lr=lr)
 8     criterion = nn.CrossEntropyLoss()
 9     for epoch in range(epochs):|
10         for i, (images, labels) in enumerate(trainLoader):
11             optimiser.zero_grad()
12             outputs = model(images.view(-1, 28*28))
13             loss = criterion(outputs, labels)
14             loss.backward()
15             optimiser.step()
16     print('Accuracy: {0:.4f}'.format(accuracy(testLoader,model)))
17     print('Training time: {0:.2f}'.format(time.time() - start))
```

Hopefully, this is fairly self-explanatory. The benchmark function takes two required parameters: the data and the model to be evaluated. We set default values for epochs and the learning rate. We need to initialize the model so we can run it more than once at a time on the same model, otherwise the model parameters will accumulate, distorting our results. The running code is identical to the code used for the previous models. Finally, we print out the accuracy and the time taken to train. The training time calculated here is really only an approximate measure, since training time will be affected by whatever else is going on on in the processor, the amount of memory, and other factors beyond our control. We should only use this result as a relative indication of a model's time performance. Finally, we need a function to calculate the accuracy, and this is defined as follows:

```
 1 def accuracy(testLoader,model):
 2     correct, total = 0, 0
 3     with torch.no_grad():
 4         for data in testLoader:
 5             images, labels = data
 6             outputs| = model(images.view(-1, 28*28))
 7             _, predicted = torch.max(outputs.data, 1)
 8             total += labels.size(0)
 9             correct += (predicted == labels).sum().item()
10     return(correct / total)
```

Remember to load the training and test datasets and make them iterable exactly as we did before. Now, we can run our three models and compare them using something like the following:

```
1 print('ReLU actiavtion:')
2 benchmark trainLoader, model4_1, epochs=5, lr = 0.1 |
3 print('Tanh activation')
4 benchmark(trainLoader, model4_2, epochs=5, lr = 0.1)
5 print('sigmoid activation')
6 benchmark(trainLoader, model4_3, epochs=5, lr = 0.1)
```

```
ReLU actiavtion:
Accuracy: 0.9575
Training time: 36.56
Tanh activation
Accuracy: 0.9516
Training time: 39.04
sigmoid activation
Accuracy: 0.9199
Training time: 38.46
```

We can see that both the `Tanh` and `ReLU` functions perform significantly better than `sigmoid`. For most networks, the `ReLU activation` function on hidden layers give the best results, both in terms of accuracy and the time it takes to train. The `ReLU` activation is not used on output layers. For the output layers, since we need to calculate the loss, we use the `softmax` function. This is the criterion for the loss class and, as before, we use `CrossEntropy Loss()`, which, if you remember, includes the `softmax` function.

There are several ways we can improve from here; one obvious way is simply to add more layers. This is typically done by adding alternating pairs of nonlinear and linear layers. In the following, we use `nn.Sequential` to organize our layers. In our forward layer, we simply have to call sequential objects, rather than every individual layer and function. This makes our code more compact and easier to read:

```
class Model4_4 nn.Module :
    def __init__(self):
        super(Model4_4b, self).__init__()
        self.layer1=nn.Sequential(nn.Linear(784, 100),
            nn.ReLU())
        self.layer2=nn.Sequential(nn.Linear(100, 50),
            nn.ReLU(),
            nn.Linear(50, 10))

    def forward(self, x):
        out = self.layer1(x)
        out = self.layer2(out)
        return out

model4_4b = Model4_4b()
```

Here, we add two more layers: a linear layer and a nonlinear ReLU layer. It is particularly important how we set the input and output sizes. In the first linear layer, the input size is 784, this is the image size. The output of this layer, something we choose, is set to 100. The input to the second linear layer, therefore, must be 100. This is the width, the number of kernels and feature maps, of the output. The output of the second linear layer is something we choose, but the general idea is to decrease the size, since we are trying to filter down the features to just 10, our target classes. For fun, create some models and try out different input and output sizes, remembering that the input to any layer must be the same size as the output of the previous layer. The following is the output of three models, where we print the output sizes of each of the hidden layers to give you an idea of what is possible:

```
3 Linear layers 100 - 50 - 10:
Accuracy: 0.9667
Training time: 38.98
3 Linear layers 1000 -100 - 10:
Accuracy: 0.9724
Training time: 71.02
4 Linear layers 1000 - 500 -50 - 10 :
Accuracy: 0.9773
Training time: 90.86
```

We can continue to add as many layers and kernels as we desire, however this is not always a good idea. How we set up input and output sizes in a network is intimately connected to the size, shape, and complexity of the data. For simple datasets, such as MNIST, it is pretty clear that a few linear layers gets very good results. At some point, simply adding linear layers, and increasing the number of kernels will not capture the highly nonlinear features of complex datasets.

Convolutional networks

So far, we have used fully connected layers in our networks, where each input unit represents a pixel in an image. With convolutional networks, on the other hand, each input unit is assigned a small localized **receptive field**. The idea of the receptive field, like ANNs themselves, is modelled on the human brain. In 1958, it was discovered that neurons in the visual cortex of the brain respond to stimuli in a limited region of a field of vision. More intriguing is that sets of neurons respond exclusively to certain basic shapes. For example, a set of neurons may respond to horizontal lines, while others respond only to lines at other orientations. It was observed that sets of neurons could have the same receptive field, but respond to different shapes. It was also noticed that neurons were organized into layers with deeper layers responding to more complex patterns. This, it turns out, is a remarkably effective way for a computer to learn and categorize a set of images.

A single convolutional layer

Convolutional layers are organized so the units in the first layer only respond to their respective receptive fields. Each unit in the next layer is connected only to a small region of the first layer, and each unit in the second hidden layer is connected to a limited region in the third layer, and so on. In this way, the network can be trained to assemble higher level features from the low-level features present in the previous layer.

In practice, this works by using a **filter**, or **convolution kernel**, to scan an image to generate what is known as a **feature map**. The kernel is just a matrix that is the size of the receptive field. We can think of this as a camera scanning an image in discrete strides. We calculate a feature map matrix by an element-wise multiplication of the kernel matrix with the values in the receptive field of an image. The resultant matrix is then summed to compute a single number in the feature map. The values in the kernel matrix represent a feature we want to extract from the image. These are the parameters that we ultimately want the model to learn. Consider a simple example where we are attempting to detect horizontal and vertical lines in an image. To simplify things, we will use one input dimension; this is either black, represented by a **1**, or white, represented by a **0**. Remember that in practice these would be scaled and normalized floating-point numbers representing a grayscale or color value. Here, we set the kernel to 4 x 4 pixels and we scan using a stride of **1**. A stride is simply the distance we move the kernel, so a stride of **1** moves the kernel one pixel:

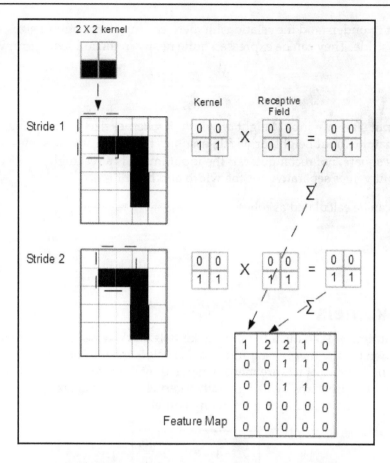

One convolution is one complete scan of the image and each convolution generates a feature map. On each stride, we do an element-wise multiplication of the kernel with the receptive field of the image and we sum the resulting matrix.

You will notice that as we move the kernel across the image, as shown in the preceding diagram, **stride 1** samples the top-left corner, **stride 2** samples the patch-one pixel to the left, **stride 3** would sample one pixel to the left again, and so on. When we reach the end of the first row, we need to add a padding pixel, so set the value to **0** in order to sample the edges of the image. Padding input data with zeros is called **valid padding**. If we did not pad the image, the feature map would be smaller, in dimensions, than the original image. Padding is used to ensure that there is no loss of information from the original.

It is important to understand the relationship between input and output sizes, kernel size, padding, and stride. They can be expressed quite neatly in the following formula:

$$O = \frac{W - K + 2P}{S} + 1$$

Here, O = output size, W = input height or width, K = kernel size, P = padding, and S = stride. Note that the input height, or width, assumes these two are the same—that is, the input image is square, not rectangular. If the input image is a rectangle, we need to calculate output values separately for the width and height.

The padding can be calculated as follows:

$$P = \frac{K - 1}{2}$$

Multiple kernels

In each convolution, we can include multiple kernels. Each kernel in a convolution generates its own feature map. The number of kernels is the number of output channels, which is also the number of feature maps generated by the convolutional layer. We can generate further feature maps by using another kernel. As an exercise, calculate the feature map that would be generated by the following kernel:

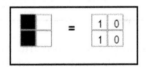

By stacking kernels, or filters, and using kennels of different sizes and values, we can extract a variety of features from an image.

Also, remember that each kernel is not restricted to one input dimension. For example, if we are processing an RGB color image, each kernel would have an input dimension of three. Since we are doing element-wise multiplication, the kernel must be the same size as the receptive field. When we have three dimensions, the kernel needs to have an input depth of three. So our greyscale 2 x 2 kernel becomes a 2 x 2 x 3 matrix for a color image. We still generate a single feature map on each convolution for each kernel. We are still able to do element-wise multiplication, since the kernel size is the same as the receptive field, except now when we do the summation, we sum across the three dimensions to get the single number required on each stride.

As you can imagine, there are a large number of ways we can scan an image. We can change the size and value of the kernel, or we can change its stride, include padding and even include noncontiguous pixels.

To get a better idea of some of the possibilities, check out vdumoulin's excellent animations: `https://github.com/vdumoulin/conv_arithmetic/blob/master/README.md`.

Multiple convolutional layers

As with the fully connected linear layers, we can add multiple convolutional layers. As with linear layers, the same restrictions apply:

- Limitations on time and memory (computational load)
- Tendency to overfit a training set and not generalize to a test set
- Requires larger datasets to work effectively

The benefit of the appropriate addition of convolution layers is that, progressively, they are able to extract more complex, nonlinear features from datasets.

Pooling layers

Convolutional layers are typically stacked using **pooling layers**. The purpose of a pooling layer is to reduce the size, but not the depth, of the feature map generated by the preceding convolution. A pooling layer retains the RGB information but compresses the spatial information. The reason we do this is to enable kernels to focus selectively on certain nonlinear features. This means we can reduce the computational load by focusing on the parameters that have the strongest influence. Having fewer parameters also reduces the tendency to overfit.

There are three major reasons why pool layers are used to reduce dimensions of the output feature map:

- Reduces computational load by discarding irrelevant features
- Smaller number of parameters, so less likely to overfit data
- Able to extract features that are transformed in some way, for example images of an object from different perspectives

Pooling layers are very similar to normal convolution layers in that they use a kernel matrix, or filter, to sample an image. The difference with pooling layers is that we downsample the input. Downsampling reduces the input dimensions. This can be achieved by either increasing the size of the kernel or increasing the stride, or both. Check the formula in the section on single convolutional layers to confirm this is true.

Remember, in a convolution all we are doing is multiplying two tensors on each stride, over an image. Each subsequent stride in a convolution samples another part of the input. This sampling is achieved by element-wise multiplication of the kernel with the output of the previous convolution layer, encompassed by that particular stride. The result of this sampling is a single number. With a convolution layer, this single number is the sum of the element-wise multiplication. With a pooling layer, this single number is typically generated by either the average or the maximum of the element-wise multiplication. The terms **average pooling** and **max** pooling refer to these different pooling techniques.

Building a single-layer CNN

So now we should have enough theory to build a simple convolution network and understand how it works. Here is a model class template we can start with:

```
1  class CNNModel1(nn.Module):
2      def __init__(self):
3          super(CNNModel1, self).__init__()
4          self.cnn1 = nn.Conv2d(in_channels=1, out_channels=32, kernel_size=5, stride=1, padding=2)
5          self.relu1 = nn.ReLU()
6          self.maxpool1 = nn.MaxPool2d(kernel_size=2)
7          self.fc1 = nn.Linear(32* 14 * 14, 10)
8
9      def forward(self, x):
10         out = self.cnn1(x)
11         out = self.relu1(out)
12         out = self.maxpool1(out)
13         out = out.view(out.size(0), -1)
14         out = self.fc1(out)
15         return out
16
17 model1=CNNModel1()
```

The basic convolutional unit we will be using is in PyTorch is the `nn.Conv2d` module. It is characterized by the following signature:

```
nn.Conv2d(in_channels, outs_channels, kernel_size, stride=1,
padding = 0)
```

The values of these parameters are constrained by the size of the input data and the formulae discussed in the last section. In this example, `in_channels` is set to 1. This refers to the fact that our input image has one color dimension. If we were working with a three-channel color image, this would be set to 3. `out_channel` is the number of kernels. We can set this to anything, but remember there are computational penalties, and improved performance is dependant on having larger, more complex datasets. For this example, we set the number of output channels to 16. The number of output channels, or kernels, is essentially the number of low-level features we think might be indicative of the target class. We set the stride to 1 and the padding to 2. This ensures the output size remains the same as the input; this can be verified by plugging these values into the output formula in the section on single convolutional layers.

In the __init__ method, you will notice we instantiate a convolutional layer, a ReLU activation function, a `MaxPool2d` layer, and a fully connected linear layer. The important thing here is to understand how we derive the values we pass to the `nn.Linear()` function. This is the output size of the MaxPool layer. We can calculate this using our output formula. We know that the output from the convolutional layer is the same as the input. Because the input image is square, we can use 28, the height or width, to represent the input, and consequently the output size of the convolutional layer. We also know that we have set a kernel size of 2. By default, `MaxPool2d` assigns the stride to the kernel size and uses implied padding. For practical purposes, this means that when we use default values for stride and padding, we can simply divide the input, here 28, by the kernel size. Since our kernel size is 2, we can calculate an output size of 14. Since we are using a fully connected linear layer, we need to flatten the width, height, and the number of channels. We have 32 channels, as set in the `out_channels` parameter of `nn.Conv2d`. Therefore, the input size is 16 X 14 X 14. The output size is 10 because, as with the linear networks, we use the output to distinguish between the 10 classes.

The `forward` function of the model is fairly straightforward. We simply pass the `out` variable through the convolutional layer, the activation function, the pooling layer, and the fully connected linear layer. Notice that we need to resize the input for the linear layer. Assuming the batch size is 100, the output of the pooling layer is a four-dimensional tensor: 100, 32, 14, 14. Here, `out.view(out.size(0), -1)` reshapes this four-dimensional tensor to a two-dimensional tensor: 100, 32*14*14.

To make this a little more concrete, let's train our model and look at a few variables. We can use almost identical code to train the convolutional model. We do, however, need to change one line in our `benchmark()` function. Since convolution layers can accept multiple input dimensions, we do not need to flatten the width and height of the input. For the previous linear models, in our running code, we used the following to flatten the input:

```
outputs= model(images.view(-1, 28*28))
```

For our convolutional layer, we do not need to do this; we can simply pass the model the image, as in the following:

```
outputs = model(images)
```

This line must also be changed in the `accuracy()` function we defined in the section on bench marking earlier in this chapter.

Building a multiple-layer CNN

As you would expect, we can improve this result by adding another convolutional layer. When we are adding multiple layers, it is convenient to bundle each layer into a sequence. It is here that `nn.Sequential` comes in handy:

```
1 class CNNModel2(nn.Module):
2     def __init__(self):
3         super(CNNModel2, self).__init__()
4         self.layer1 = nn.Sequential(
5             nn.Conv2d(1, 16, kernel_size=5, stride=1, padding=2),
6             nn.ReLU(),
7             nn.MaxPool2d(kernel_size=2, stride=2))
8
9         self.layer2 = nn.Sequential(
10            nn.Conv2d(16, 32, kernel_size=5, stride=1, padding=2),
11            nn.ReLU(),
12            nn.MaxPool2d(kernel_size=2, stride=2))
13        self.lin1=nn.Linear(32* 7* 7, 10)
14
15    def forward(self, x):
16        out = self.layer1(x)
17        out = self.layer2(out)
18        out = out.view(out.size(0), -1)
19        out = self.lin1(out)
20        return out
21 model2=CNNModel2()
```

We initialize two hidden layers and a fully connected linear output layer. Note the parameters passed to the `Conv2d` instances and the linear output. As before, we have one input dimension. From this, our convolutional layer outputs 16 feature maps or output channels.

This diagram represents the two-layered convolutional network:

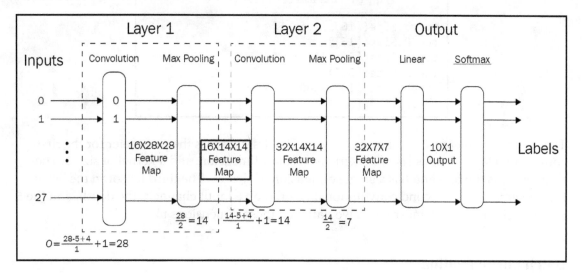

This should make it clear how we calculate the output sizes, and in particular how we derive the input size for the linear output layer. We know, using the output formula, that the output size of the first convolutional layer, before max pooling, is the same as the input size, that is 28 x 28. Since we are using 16 kernels or channels, generating 16 feature maps, the input to the max pooling layer is a 16 x 28 x 28 tensor. The max pooling layer, with a kernel size of 2, a stride of 2, and the default implicit padding means that we simply divide the feature map size by 2 to calculate the max pool out put size. This gives us an output size of 16 x 14 x 14. This is the input size to the second convolutional layer. Once again, using the output formula, we can calculate that the second convolutional layer, before max pooling, generates 14 x 14 feature maps, the same size as its input. Since we set the number of kernels to 32, the input to the second max pooling layer is a 32 x 14 x 14 matrix. Our second max pooling layer is identical to the first, with the kernel size and stride set to 2 and default implicit padding. Once again, we can simply divide by 2 to calculate the output size, and therefore the input to the linear output layer. Finally, we need to flatten this matrix to one dimension. So the input size for the linear output layer is a single dimension of 32 * 7 * 7, or 1,568. As usual, we need the output size of the final linear layer to be the number of classes, which in this case is 10.

We can inspect the model parameters to see that is exactly what is happening when we run the code:

```
1  parameters=list((model.parameters()))
2  for parameter in parameters:
3      print(parameter.size())

torch.Size([16, 1, 5, 5])
torch.Size([16])
torch.Size([32, 16, 5, 5])
torch.Size([32])
torch.Size([10, 1568])
torch.Size([10])
```

The model parameters consist of six tensors. The first tensor is the parameter for the first convolution layer. It consists of 16 kernels, 1 color dimension, and a kernel of size 5. The next tensor is the bias and has a single dimension of size 16. The third tensor in the list is the 32 kernels in the second convolutional layer, the 16 input channels, the depth, and the 5 x 5 kernel. In the final linear layer, we flattened these dimensions to 10 x 1568.

Batch normalization

Batch normalization is used widely to improve the performance of neural networks. It works by stabilizing the distributions of layer input. This is achieved by adjusting the mean and variance of these input. It is fairly indicative of the nature of deep learning research that there is uncertainty among the researcher community as to why batch normalization is so effective. It was thought that this was because it reduces the so called **internal co-variate shift** (**ICS**). This refers to the change in distributions as a result of the preceding layers' parameter updates. The original motivation for batch normalization was to reduce this shift. However, a clear link between ICS and performance has not been conclusively found. More recent research has shown that batch normalization works by *smoothing* the optimization landscape. Basically, this means that gradient descent will work more efficiently. Details of this can be found in *How Does Batch Normalization Help Optimization?* by Santurkar et al., which is available at https://arxiv.org/abs/1805.11604.

Batch normalization, implemented with the `nn.BatchNorm2d` function:

```
1  class CNNModel3(nn.Module):
2      def __init__(self):
3          super(CNNModel3, self).__init__()
4          self.layer1 = nn.Sequential(
5              nn.Conv2d(1, 16, kernel_size=5, stride=1, padding=2),
6              nn.BatchNorm2d(16),
7              nn.ReLU(),
8              nn.MaxPool2d(kernel_size=2, stride=2))
9
10         self.layer2 = nn.Sequential(
11             nn.Conv2d(16, 32, kernel_size=5, stride=1, padding=2),
12             nn.BatchNorm2d(32),
13             nn.ReLU(),
14             nn.MaxPool2d(kernel_size=2, stride=2))
15         self.lin1=nn.Linear(32* 7* 7, 10)
16
17     def forward(self, x):
18         out = self.layer1(x)
19         out = self.layer2(out)
20         out = out.view(out.size(0), -1)
21         out = self.lin1(out)
22         return out
23 model3=CNNModel3()
```

This model is identical to the previous two-layer CNN with the addition of the batch normalization of the output of the convolutional layers. The following is a printout of the performance of the three convolutional networks we have built so far:

```
Single convolutional layer accuracy: 0.9343
Training time: 234.96
Two convolutional layers accuracy: 0.9676
Training time  model2: 386.19
Two convolutional layers with batchnorm accuracy: 0.9844
Training time  model3 :471.86
```

Summary

In this chapter, we saw how we could improve the simple linear network developed in Chapter 3, *Computational Graphs and Linear Models*. We can add linear layers, increase the width of the network, increase the number of epochs we run the model, and tweak the learning rate. However, linear networks will not be able to capture the nonlinear features of datasets, and at some point their performance will plateau. Convolutional layers, on the other hand, use a kernel to learn nonlinear features. We saw that with two convolutional layers, performance on MNIST improved significantly.

In the next chapter, we'll look at some different network architectures, including recurrent networks and long short-term networks.

5
Other NN Architectures

Recurrent networks are essentially feedforward networks that retain state. All the networks we have looked at so far require an input of a fixed size, such as an image, and give a fixed size output, such as the probabilities of a particular class. Recurrent networks are different in that they accept a sequence, of arbitrary size, as the input and produce a sequence as output. Moreover, the internal state of the network's hidden layers is updated as a result of a learned function and the input. In this way, a recurrent network remembers its state. Subsequent states are a function of previous states.

In this chapter, we will cover the following:

- Introduction to recurrent networks
- Long short-term memory networks

Introduction to recurrent networks

Recurrent networks have been shown to be very powerful in predicting time series data. This is something fundamental to biological brains that enables us to do things such as safely drive a car, play a musical instrument, evade predators, understand language, and interact with a dynamic world. This sense of the flow of time and the understanding of how things change over time is fundamental to intelligent life, so it is no surprise that in artificial systems this ability is important.

The ability to understand time series data is also important in creative endeavors, and recurrent networks have shown some ability in things such as composing a melody, constructing grammatically correct sentences, and creating visually pleasing images.

Feedforward and convolutional networks achieve very good results, as we have seen, in tasks such as the classification of static images. However, working with continuous data, as is required for tasks such as speech or handwriting recognition, predicting stock market prices, or forecasting the weather requires a different approach. In these types of tasks, both the input and the output are no longer a fixed size of data, but a sequence of arbitrary length.

Recurrent artificial neurons

For artificial neurons in feedforward networks, the flow of activation is simply from the input to the output. **Recurrent artificial neurons (RANs)** have a connection from the output of the activation layer to its linear input, essentially summing the output back into the input. A RAN can be *unrolled* in time: each subsequent state is a function of previous states. In this way, a RAN can be said to have a memory of its previous states:

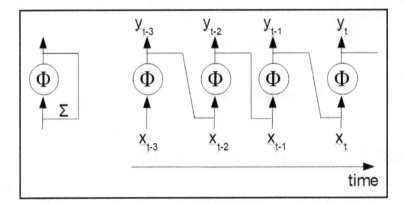

In the preceding diagram, the diagram on the left illustrates a single recurrent neuron. It sums its input, x, with the output, y, to produce a new output. The diagram on the right shows this same unit unrolled over three time steps. We can write an equation for the output with respect to the input for any given time step as follows:

$$y_{(t)} = \left(x_{(t)}^T \cdot w_x + y_{(t-1)}^T \cdot w_y + b\right)\Phi$$

Here, *y(t)* is the output vector at time *t*, *x(t)* is the input at time *t*, *y(t-1)* is the output of the previous time step, *b* is the bias term, and *Φ* is the activation, usually tanh or RelU. Notice that each unit has two sets of weights, w_x and w_y, for the inputs and the outputs respectively. This is, essentially, the formula we used for our linear networks with an added term to represent the output, fed back into the input at time *t-1*.

In the same way that with CNNs (Convolutional Neural Networks) we could compute the outputs of an entire layer over a batch, using a vectorized form of the previous equation, this is also possible with recurrent networks. The following is the vectorized form for a recurrent layer:

$$Y_{(t)} = (X_{(t)} . W_x + Y_{(t-1)} . W_y + b)\Phi$$

Here, $Y_{(t)}$ is the output at time t. This is a matrix of size (m, n), where m is the number of instances in the batch and n is the number of units in the layer. $X_{(t)}$ is a matrix of size (m, i) where i is the number of input features. W_x is a matrix of size (i, n), containing the input weights of the current time step. W_y is a matrix of size (n, n), containing the weights of the outputs for the previous time step.

Implementing a recurrent network

So we can concentrate on the models, we will use the same dataset we are familiar with. Even though we are working with static images, we can treat these as a time series by unrolling each 28 pixel input size over 28 time steps, enabling the network to make a computation on the complete image:

```
1  class Model5_1(nn.Module):
2      def __init__(self):
3          inSize=28
4          hiddenSize=100
5          numLayers=2
6          outSize = 10
7          super(Model5_1, self).__init__()
8          self.rnn = nn.RNN(inSize, hiddenSize, numLayers, batch_first=True)
9          self.fc = nn.Linear(hiddenSize, outSize)
10
11     def forward(self, x):
12         h0 = torch.zeros(numLayers, x.size(0), hiddenSize)
13         out, hn = self.rnn(x, h0)
14         out = self.fc(out[:, -1, :])
15         return out
16
17 model5_1 = Model5_1()
```

In the preceding model, we use the nn.RNN class to create a model with two recurrent layers. The nn.RNN class has the following default signature:

```
nn.RNN(input_size, hidden_size, num_layers, batch_first=False, nonlinearity
= 'tanh'
```

The input is our 28 x 28 MNIST images. This model takes 28 pixels of each image, unrolling them over 28 time steps to make a computation over the entirety of all images in the batch. The hidden_size parameter is the dimension of the hidden layers, and this is something we choose. Here, we use a size of 100. The batch_first parameter specifies the expected shape of the input and output tensors. We want this to have the shape in the form of (batch, sequence, features). In this example, the expected input/output tensor shape we want is (100, 28, 28). That is the batch size, the length of the sequence, and the number of features at each step; however, by default the nn.RNN class uses input/output tensors of the form (sequence, batch, features). Setting batch_first = True ensures the input/output tensors are of the shape (batch, sequence, features).

In the forward method, we initialize a tensor for the hidden layer, h0, that is updated on every iteration of the model. The shape of this hidden tensor, representing the hidden state, is of the form (layers, batch, hidden). In this example, we have two layers. The second dimension of the hidden state is the batch size. Remember, we are using batch first so this is the first dimension of the input tensor, x, indexed using x[0]. The final dimension is the hidden size, which in this example we have set to 100.

The nn.RNN class requires an input consisting of the input tensor, x, and the h0 hidden state. This is why in the forward method, we pass in these two variables. The forward method is called once every iteration, updating the hidden state and giving an output. Remember, number of iterations is the number of epochs multiplied by the data size divided by the batch size.

Importantly, as you can see, we need to index the output using the following:

```
out = self.fc(out[:, -1, :])
```

We are only interested in the output of the last time step, since this is the accumulated knowledge of all the images in the batch. If you remember, the output shape is of the form (batch, sequence, features) and in our model this is (100, 28, 100). The number of features is simply the number of hidden dimensions or number of units in the hidden layer. Now, we require all batches: this is why we use the colon as the first index. Here, -1 indicates we only want the last element of the sequence. The last index, the colon, indicates we want all of the features. Hence, our output is all the features of the last time step in the sequence, for one entire batch.

We can use almost identical training code; however, we do need to reshape the output when we call the model. Remember that for linear models, we reshaped the output using the following:

```
outputs = model(images.view(-1, 28*28)
```

For convolution networks, by using nn.CNN we could pass in the unflattened image and for recurrent networks, when using nn.RNN we need the output to be of the form (batch, sequence, features). Therefore, we can use the following to reshape the output:

```
outputs = model(images.view(-1, 28,28))
```

Remember, we need to change this line in both our training code and testing code. The following printout is the result of running three recurrent models using different layer and hidden size configurations:

```
2 layers, hidden size 100
Accuracy: 0.9473
Training time: 235.75

 2 layers, hidden size 200
Accuracy: 0.9675
Training time: 497.41

 3 layers, hidden size 200
Accuracy: 0.9717
Training time: 804.50
```

To get a better understanding of how this model works, consider the following diagram, representing our two-layer model with a hidden size of `100`:

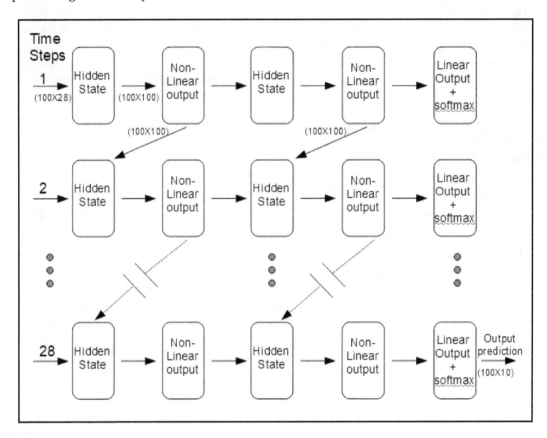

At each of the **28** time steps the network takes an input, consisting of **28** pixels—the features—from each of the images in the **100** image batch. Each of the time steps are basically a two-layer feedforward network. The only difference is that there is an extra input to each of the hidden layers. This input consists of the output from the equivalent layer in the previous time step. At each time step, another **28** pixels are sampled from each of the **100** images in the batch. Finally, when the entirety of all the images in the batch have been processed, the weights of the model are updated and the next iteration begins. Once all iterations are complete, we read the output to obtain a prediction.

To get a better understanding of what happens when we run the code, consider the following:

```
1 for i in range(len(list(model5_1.parameters()))):
2                 print(list(model5_1.parameters())[i].size())

torch.Size([100, 28])
torch.Size([100, 100])
torch.Size([100])
torch.Size([100])
torch.Size([100, 100])
torch.Size([100, 100])
torch.Size([100])
torch.Size([100])
torch.Size([10, 100])
torch.Size([10])
```

Here, we print out the size of the weight vectors for a two-layer RNN model with a hidden layer size of 100.

We retrieve the weights as a list containing 10 tensors. The first tensor of size [100, 28] consists of the inputs to the hidden layer, 100 units, and the 28 features, or pixels, of the input images. This is the W_x term in the vectorized form equation of the recurrent network. The next group of parameters, size [100, 100], represented by the W_y term in the preceding equation, is the output weights of the hidden layer, consisting of the 100 units each of size 100. The next two single-dimension tensors, each of size 100, are the bias units of the input and the hidden layer respectively. Next, we have the input weights, output weights, and biases of the second layer. Finally, we have the read out layer weights, a tensor of size [10, 100], for 10 possible predictions using 100 features. The final single-dimension tensor of size [10] includes the bias units for the read out layer.

In the following code, we have replicated what is happening in the recurrent layers of our model over a single batch of images:

```
1 dataiter = iter(trainLoader)
2 images, labels = dataiter.next()
3 rnn = nn.RNN(28,100, 2, batch_first=True)
4 h0 = torch.zeros(2, images.size(0), 100)
5 output, hn = rnn(images.view(-1, 28,28), h0)
```

You can see that we have simply created an iterator out of the `trainLoader` dataset object and assigned an `images` variable to a batch of images, as we did for our training code. The hidden layer, h0, needs to contain two tensors, one for each layer. In each of these tensors, for each image in the batch, the weights of the 100 hidden units are stored. This explains why we need a three-dimensional tensor. The first dimension of size 2 for the number of layers, the second dimension is of size 100 for the batch size, obtained from `images.size(0)`, and the third dimension is of size 100 for the number of hidden units. We then pass a reshaped image tensor and our hidden tensor to the model. This calls the model's `forward()` function, making the necessary computations, and returning two tensors an output tensor, and an updated hidden state tensor.

The following confirms these output sizes:

```
1 output.size()
torch.Size([100, 28, 100])

1 hn.size()
torch.Size([2, 100, 100])

1 images.size()
torch.Size([100, 1, 28, 28])

1 images.view(-1, 28,28).size()
torch.Size([100, 28, 28])
```

This should help you understand why we need to resize the `images` tensor. Note that the features for the input are the 28 pixels for each of the images in the batch, which are unrolled over the sequence of 28 time steps. Next, let's pass the output of the recurrent layer to our fully connected linear layer:

```
1 fc=nn.Linear(100,10)
2 output2=fc output[:, -1, :]

1 output2.size()
torch.Size([100, 10])
```

You can see that this will give us 10 predictions for each of the 100 features present in the output. This is why we need to index only the last element in the sequence. Remember the output from nn.RNN is of size (100, 28, 100). Note what happens to the size of this tensor when we index it using -1:

```
1 output[:, -1, :].size()
torch.Size([100, 100])
```

This is the tensor containing the 100 features, the outputs of the hidden units, for each of the 100 images in the batch. This is passed to our linear layer to give the required 10 predictions for each image.

Long short-term memory networks

Long short-term memory networks (LSTMS), are a special type of RNN capable of learning long-term dependencies. While standard RNNs can remember previous states to some extent, they did this on a fairly basic level by updating a hidden state on each time step. This enabled the network to remember short-term dependencies. The hidden state, being a function of previous states, retains information about these previous states. However, the more time steps there are between the current state and a previous state, it diminishes the effect that this earlier state will have on the current state. Far less information is retained on a state that is say 10 time steps before the time step immediately preceding the current step. This is despite that fact that earlier time steps may contain important information with direct relevance to a particular problem or task we are trying to solve.

Biological brains have a remarkable ability to remember long-term dependencies, forming meaning and understanding using these dependencies. Consider how we follow the plot of a movie. We recall events that occurred at the beginning of the movie and immediately understand their relevance as the plot develops. Not only that, but we can apply context to the movie by recalling events in our own lives that give relevance and meaning to a story line. This ability to selectively apply memories to current context, yet at the same time filter out irrelevant details, is the strategy behind the design of LSTMs.

An LSTM network is an attempt to incorporate these long-term dependencies into an artificial network. It is considerably more complex than a standard RNN; however, it is still based on recurrent feedforward networks and understanding this theory should enable you to understand LSTMs.

The following diagram shows an LSTM over one single time step:

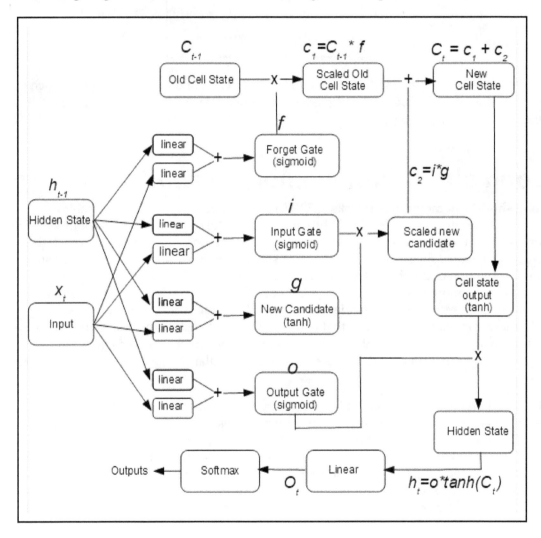

As with normal RNNs, each subsequent time step takes the hidden state of the previous time step, h_{t-1}, along with the data, x_t, as its input. An LSTM also passes on a cell state that is calculated on each time step. You can see that h_{t-1} and x_t are each passed to four separate linear functions. Each pair of these linear functions is summed. Central to an LSTM are the four gates that these summations are passed in to. First, we have the **Forget Gate**. This uses a **sigmoid** for activation and is element-wise multiplied by the **Old Cell State**. Remember the **sigmoid** is effectively squashing the **linear** output values to values between zero and one. Multiplying by zero will effectively eliminate that particular value in the cell state and multiplying by one will keep this value. The **Forget Gate** essentially decides what information is passed to the next time step. This is achieved by element-wise multiplication with the **Old Cell State**.

The **Input Gate** and the **Scaled new candidate** gate together determine what information is retained. The **Input Gate** also uses a **sigmoid** function and this is multiplied by the output of a **New Candidate** gate, creating a temporary tensor, the **Scaled new candidate**, c_2. Note that the **New Candidate** gate uses **tanh** activation. Remember the **tanh** function outputs a value between –1 and 1. Using **tanh** and **sigmoid** activation in such a way—that is, by element-wise multiplication of their outputs—helps prevent the vanishing gradient problem, where outputs become saturated and their gradients repeatedly become close to zero, making them unable to perform meaningful computations. A **New Cell State** is calculated by summing the **Scaled new candidate** with the **Scaled Old Cell State**, and in this way is able to amplify important components of the input data.

The final gate, the output gate, **O**, is another **sigmoid**. The new cell state is passed through a **tanh** function and this is element-wise multiplied by the output gate to calculate the **Hidden State**. This **Hidden State**, as with standard RNNs, is passed through a final non-linearity, a **sigmoid**, and a **Softmax** function to give the outputs. This has the overall effect of reinforcing high energy components, eliminating the lower energy components, as well as reducing the opportunities for vanishing gradients and reducing overfitting of the training set.

We can write the equations for each of the LSTM gates as follows:

$$f = sigmoid(w_1 x_t + b_1 + w_2 h_{t-1} + b_2)$$

$$i = sigmoid(w_3 x_t + b_3 + w_4 h_{t-1} + b_4)$$

$$g = tanh(w_5 x_t + b_5 + w_6 h_{t-1} + b_6)$$

$$o = sigmoid(w_7 x_t + b_7 + w_8 h_{t-1} + b_8)$$

Notice that these equations have an identical form to those of the RNN. The only difference is that we require eight separate weight tensors and eight bias tensors. It is these extra weight dimensions that give LSTMs their extra ability to learn and retain important features of the input data, as well as discard less important features. We can write the output of the linear output layer, of a particular time step, t, as the following:

$$O_t = w_9 h_1 + b_9$$

Implementing an LSTM

The following is the LSTM model class we will use for MNIST:

```
1  class Model5_3(nn.Module):
2      def __init__(self):
3          super(Model5_3, self).__init__()
4          self.inSize=28
5          self.hiddenSize=100
6          self.numLayers=2
7          self.outSize = 10
8          self.lstm = nn.LSTM(self.inSize, self.hiddenSize, self.numLayers, batch_first=True)
9          self.fc = nn.Linear(self.hiddenSize, self.outSize)
10
11     def forward(self, x):
12         h0 = torch.zeros(self.numLayers, x.size(0), self.hiddenSize)
13         c0 = torch.zeros(self.numLayers, x.size(0), self.hiddenSize)
14         out, (hn, cn) = self.lstm(x, (h0,c0))
15         out = self.fc(out[:, -1, :])
16         return out
17
18 model5_3 = Model5_3()
```

Notice that nn.LSTM is passed the same arguments as the previous RNN. This is not surprising, since LSTM is a recurrent network that works on sequences of data. Remember the input tensor has an axis of the form (batch, sequence, feature), so we set batch_first = True. We initialize a fully connected linear layer for the output layer. Notice in the forward method that, as well as initializing a hidden state tensor, h0, we also initialize a tensor to hold the cell state, c0. Remember also the out tensor contains all 28 time steps. For our prediction, we are only interested in the last index in the sequence. This is why we apply the [:, -1, :] indexing to the out tensor before passing it to the linear output layer. We can print out the parameters for this model in the same way as for the RNN previously:

```
1  for i in range(len(list(model5_2.parameters()))):
2              print(list(model5_2.parameters())[i].size())
```
```
torch.Size([400, 28])
torch.Size([400, 100])
torch.Size([400])
torch.Size([400])
torch.Size([10, 100])
torch.Size([10])
```

These are the parameters for a single-layer LSTM with 100 hidden layers. There are six groups of parameters for this single-layer LSTM. Notice that instead of the input and hidden weight tensors having a size of 100 in the first dimension, as was the case for the RNN, for an LSTM, this is a size of 400, representing 100 hidden units for each of the four LSTM gates.

The first parameter tensor is for the input layer and is of size [400, 28]. The first index, 400, corresponds to the weights w_1, w_3, w_5, and w_7, each of which is of size 100, for the inputs into the 100 hidden units specified. The 28 is the number of features, or pixels, present at the input. The next tensor, of size [400, 100], are the weights w_2, w_4, w_6, and w_8 for each of 100 hidden units. The following two single-dimension tensors of size [400] are the two sets of bias units, b_1, b_3, b_5, b_7 and b_2, b_4, b_6, b_8, for each of the LSTM gates. Finally, we have the output tensor of size [10, 100]. This is our output size, 10, and the weight tensor w_9. The last single-dimension tensor of size [10] is the bias, $b9$.

Building a language model with a gated recurrent unit

To demonstrate the flexibility of recurrent networks, we are going to do something different in the final section of this chapter. Up until now, we have been working with probably the most-used testing data set, MNIST. This dataset has characteristics that are well known and it is extremely useful for comparing different types of models and testing different architectures and parameter sets. However, there are some tasks, such as natural language processing, that quite obviously require an entirely different type of dataset.

Also, the models we have built so far have been focused on one simple task: classification. This is the most straightforward machine learning task. To give you a flavor of other machine learning tasks, and to demonstrate the potential of recurrent networks, the model we are going to build is a character-based prediction model that attempts to predict each subsequent character based on the previous character, forming a learned body of text. The model first learns to create correct vowel—consonant sequences, words, and eventually sentences and paragraphs that mimic the form (but not the meaning) of those constructed by human authors.

The following is an adaption of code written by Sean Robertson and Pratheek that can be found here: `https://github.com/spro/practical-pytorch/blob/master/char-rnn-generation/char-rnn-generation.ipynb`. Here is the model definition:

```python
1  class Model5_2(nn.Module):
2      def __init__(self, numCharacters):
3          super(Model5_2, self).__init__()
4          self.input_size = numCharacters
5          self.hidden_size = 100
6          self.output_size = numCharacters
7          self.n_layers = 2
8
9          self.encoder = nn.Embedding(numCharacters, hidden_size)
10         self.gru = nn.GRU(hidden_size, hidden_size, n_layers)
11         self.decoder = nn.Linear(hidden_size, numCharacters)
12
13     def forward(self, input, hidden):
14         input = self.encoder(input.view(1, -1))
15         output, hidden = self.gru(input.view(1, 1, -1), hidden)
16         output = self.decoder(output.view(1, -1))
17         return output, hidden
18
19     def init_hidden(self):
20         return torch.zeros(self.n_layers, 1, self.hidden_size)
```

The purpose of this model is to take an input character at each time step, and output the most likely next character. Over subsequent training, it begins to build up sequences of characters that mimic text from a training sample. Our input and output sizes are simply the number of characters in the input text, and this is calculated and passed in as a parameter to the model. We initialize an encoder tensor using the nn.Embedding class. In a similar way to how we used one hot encoding to define a unique index for each word, the nn.Embedding module stores each word in a vocabulary as a multidimensional tensor. This enables us to encode semantic information in the word embedding. We need to pass the nn.Embedding module a vocabulary size—here, this is the number of characters in the input text—and a dimensionality in which to encode each character—here, this is the hidden size of the model.

The word embedding model we are using is based on the nn.GRU module, or GRU. This is very similar to the LSTM module we used in the previous section. The difference is that GRU is a slightly simplified version of LSTM. It combines the input and forget gates into a single update gate, and combines the hidden state with the cell state. The result is that the GRU is more efficient than LSTM for many tasks. Finally, a linear output layer is initialized to decode the output from the GRU. In the forward method, we resize the input and pass it through the linear embedding layer, the GRU, and the final linear output layer, returning the hidden state and the output.

Next, we need to import the data, and initialize variables containing the printable characters of our input text and the number of characters in the input text. Note the use of `unidecode` to remove non-unicode characters. You will need to import this module and possibly install it on your system if it is not installed already. We also define two convenience functions: a function to convert a character string into the integer equivalent of each Unicode character, and another function to sample random chunks of training text. The `random_training_set` function returns two tensors. The `inp` tensor contains all characters in the chunk, excluding the last character. The `target` tensor contains all elements of the chunk offset by one and so includes the last character. For example, if we were using a chunk size of 4, and this chunk consisted of the Unicode character representations of [41, 27, 29, 51], then the `inp` tensor would be [41, 27, 29] and the `target` tensor [27, 29, 51]. In this way, the target can train a model to make a prediction on the next character using target data:

```
1  allCharacters = string.printable
2  numCharacters = len(allCharacters)
3  file = unidecode.unidecode(open('data/warandpeace.txt').read())
4  chunk_len = 200
5
6  def char_tensor(string):
7      tensor = torch.zeros(len(string)).long().unsqueeze(1)
8      for c in range(len(string)):
9          tensor[c] = allCharacters.index(string[c])
10     return tensor
11
12 def random_training_set():
13     start_index = random.randint(0, len(file) - chunk_len)
14     end_index = start_index + chunk_len + 1
15     chunk = file[start_index:end_index]
16     inp = char_tensor(chunk[:-1])
17     target = char_tensor(chunk[1:])
18     return inp, target
```

Next, we write a method to evaluate the model. This is done by passing it one character at a time: the model outputs a multinomial probability distribution for the next most likely character. This is repeated to build up a sequence of characters, storing them in the `predicted` variable:

```
1 def evaluate(prime_str='A', predict_len=500, temperature=0.8):
2     hidden = decoder.init_hidden()
3     prime_input = char_tensor(prime_str)
4     predicted = prime_str
5
6     for p in range(len(prime_str) - 1):
7         _, hidden = decoder(prime_input[p], hidden)
8     inp = prime_input[-1]
9
10    for p in range(predict_len):
11        output, hidden = decoder(inp, hidden)
12        output_dist = output.data.view(-1).div(temperature).exp()
13        top_i = torch.multinomial(output_dist, 1)[0]
14        predicted_char = allCharacters[top_i]
15        predicted += predicted_char
16        inp = char_tensor(predicted_char)
17    return predicted
```

The `evaluate` function takes a `temperature` argument that divides the output and finds the exponent to create a probability distribution. The `temperature` argument has the effect of determining the level of probability required for each prediction. For temperature values above 1, characters with lower probabilities are generated, the resulting text being more random. For lower temperature values below 1, higher probability characters are generated. With temperature values close to 0, only the most likely characters will be generated. For each iteration, a character is added to the `predicted` string until the required length, determined by the `predict_len` variable, is reached and the `predicted` string is returned.

The following function trains the model:

```
1  def train(inp, target):
2      hidden = decoder.init_hidden()
3      decoder.zero_grad()
4      loss = 0
5
6      for c in range(chunk_len):
7          output, hidden = decoder(inp[c], hidden)
8          loss += criterion output, target[c]
9
10     loss.backward()
11     decoder_optimizer.step()
12     return loss.item() / chunk_len
```

We pass it the input chunk and the target chunk. The `for` loop runs the model through one iteration for each character in the chunk, updating the `hidden` state and returning the average loss for each character.

Now, we are ready to instantiate and run the model. This is done with the following code:

```
1  n_epochs = 1000
2  print_every = 50
3  hidden_size = 100
4  n_layers = 2
5  lr = 0.01
6
7  decoder = Model5_2(numCharacters)
8  decoder_optimizer = torch.optim.Adam(decoder.parameters(), lr=lr)
9  criterion = nn.CrossEntropyLoss()
10 loss_avg = 0
11
12 for epoch in range(1, n_epochs + 1):
13     loss = train(*random_training_set())
14     loss_avg += loss
15     if epoch % print_every == 0:
16         print('Epoch: {0:1d} Loss: {1:.4f}'.format(epoch, loss))
17         print(evaluate('but', 100), '\n')
```

Here, the usual variables are initialized. Notice that we are not using stochastic gradient descent for our optimizer, but rather use the Adam optimizer. The term Adam stands for *adaptive moment estimator*. Gradient descent uses a single fixed learning rate for all learnable parameters. The Adam optimizer uses an adaptive learning rate that maintains a per parameter learning rate. It can improve learning efficiency, particularly in sparse representations such as those used for natural language processing. Sparse representations are those where most of the values in a tensor are zero, for example in one-hot encoding or word embeddings.

Once we run the model, it will print out the predicted text. At first, the text appears as almost random sequences of characters; however, after a few cycles of training, the model learns to format the text into English-like sentences and phrases. Generative models are powerful tools, enabling us to uncover probability distributions in input data.

Summary

In this chapter, we introduced recurrent neural networks and demonstrated how to use an RNN on the MNIST dataset. RNNs are particularly useful for working with time series data, since they are essentially feedforward networks that are unrolled over time. This makes them very suitable for tasks such as handwriting and speech recognition, as they operate on sequences of data. We also looked at a more powerful variant of the RNN, the LSTM. The LSTM uses four gates to decide what information to pass on to the next time step, enabling it to uncover long-term dependencies in data. Finally, in this chapter we built a simple language model, enabling us to generate text from sample input text. We used a model based on the GRU. The GRU is a slightly simplified version of the LSTM, containing three gates and combining the input and forget gates of the LSTM. This model used probability distributions to generate text from a sample input.

In the final chapter, we will examine some advanced features of PyTorch, such as using PyTorch in multiprocessor and distributed environments. We also see how to fine-tune PyTorch models and use pre-trained models for flexible image classification.

Getting the Most out of PyTorch

6

By now, you should be able to build and train three different types of model: linear, convolutional, and recurrent. You should have an appreciation of the theory and mathematics behind these model architectures and explain how they make predictions. Convolutional networks are probably the most studied deep learning network, especially in relation to image data. Of course, both convolutional and recurrent networks make extensive use of linear layers, so the theory behind linear networks, most notably linear regression and gradient descent, is fundamental to all artificial neural networks.

Our discussion so far has been fairly contained. We have looked at a well-studied problem, such as classification using MNIST, to give you a solid understanding of the basic PyTorch building blocks. This final chapter is the launching pad for your use of PyTorch in the real world, and after reading it you should be well placed to begin your own deep learning exploration. In this chapter, we will discuss the following topics:

- Using **graphics processing units** (**GPUs**) to improve performance
- Optimization strategies and techniques
- Using pretrained models

Multiprocessor and distributed environments

There are a variety of multiprocessor and distributed environment possibilities. The most common reason for using more than one processor is, of course, to make models run faster. The time it takes to load MNIST—a relatively tiny dataset of 60,000 images—to memory is not significant. However, consider the situation where we have giga or terabytes of data, or if the data is distributed across multiple servers. The situation is even more complex when we consider online models, where data is being harvested from multiple servers in real time. Clearly, some sort of parallel processing capability is required.

Using a GPU

The simplest way to make a model run faster is to add GPUs. A significant reduction in training time can be achieved by transferring processor-intensive tasks from the **central processing unit** (**CPU**) to one or more GPUs. PyTorch uses the `torch.cuda()` module to interface with the GPUs. CUDA is a parallel computing model created by NVIDIA that features lazy assignment so that resources are only allocated when needed. The resulting efficiency gains are substantial.

PyTorch uses a context manager, `torch.device()`, to assign tensors to a particular device. The following screenshot shows an example of this:

```
import torch
w=torch.rand(3,3).to('cuda')
print(w)

tensor([[0.2629, 0.2429, 0.8316],
        [0.1465, 0.3592, 0.9654],
        [0.5141, 0.1318, 0.9772]], device='cuda:0')
```

It is a more usual practice to test for a GPU and assign a device to a variable using the following semantics:

```
device = torch.device("cuda:0" if torch.cuda.is_available() else "cpu")
```

The `"cuda:0"` string refers to the default GPU device. Note that we test for the presence of a GPU device and assign it to the `device` variable. If a GPU device is unavailable, then the device is assigned to the CPU. This allows code to run on machines that may or may not have a GPU.

Consider the linear model we explored in `Chapter 3`, *Computational Graphs and Linear Models*. We can use exactly the same model definition; however, we need to change a few things in our training code to ensure processor-intensive operations occur on the GPU. Once we have create our `device` variable, we can assign operations to that device.

In the benchmark function we created earlier, we need to add the following line of code after we initialize the model:

```
model.to(device)
```

We also need to ensure the operations on the images, labels, and outputs all occur on the selected device. In the `for` loop of the benchmark function, we make the following changes:

```
for epoch in range(epochs):
    for i, (images, labels) in enumerate(trainLoader):
        images = images.requires_grad_().to(device)
        labels = labels.to(device)
        optimiser.zero_grad()
        outputs = model(images.view(-1, 28*28)).to(device)
```

We need do to exactly the same thing for the images, labels, and outputs defined in our accuracy function, simply appending `.to(device)` to these tensor definitions. Once these changes have been made, if it is run on a system with a GPU, it should run noticeably faster. For a model with four linear layers, this code ran in just over 55 seconds, compared to over 120 seconds when run just on the CPU on my system. Of course, CPU speed, memory, and other factors contribute to running time, so these benchmarks will be different on different systems. The exact same training code will work for a logistic regression model. The same modifications also work for the training code for the other networks we have studied. Almost anything can be transferred to a GPU, but be aware that there is a computational expense incurred every time data is copied to the GPU, so do not unnecessarily transfer operations to the GPU unless a complex computation—for example, calculating a gradient—is involved.

If you have multiple GPUs available on your system, then `nn.DataParallel` can be used to transparently distribute operations across these GPUs. This can be as simple as using a wrapper around your model—for example, `model=torch.nn.DataParallel(model)`. We can of course use a more granular approach and assign specific operations to specific devices, as shown in the following example:

```
with torch.cuda.device("device:2"): w3=torch.rand(3,3)
```

PyTorch has a specific memory space available to speed up the transfer of tensors to the GPU. This is used when a tensor is repeatedly allocated to a GPU. This is achieved using the `pin_memory()` function—for example, `w3.pin_memory()`. One of the major uses for this is to speed up the loading of input data, which occurs repeatedly over a model's training cycle. To do this, simply pass the `pin_memory=True` argument to the `DataLoader` object when it is instantiated.

Distributed environments

Sometimes, data and computing resources are not available on a single physical machine. This requires protocols for exchanging tensor data over a network. With distributed environments, where computations can occur on different kinds of physical hardware over a network, there are a large number of considerations—for example, network latencies or errors, processor availability, scheduling and timing issues, and competing processing resources. In an ANN, it is essential that calculations are produced in a certain order. The complex machinery for the assigning and timing of each computation across networks of machines and processors in each machine is, thankfully, largely hidden in PyTorch using higher-level interfaces.

PyTorch has two main packages, each of which deals the various aspects of distributed and parallel environments. This is in addition to CUDA, which we discussed previously. These packages are as follows:

- `torch.distributed`
- `torch.multiprocessing`

torch.distributed

Using `torch.distributed` is probably the most common approach. This package provides communication primitives, such as classes, to check the number of nodes in a network, ensure the availability of backend communication protocols, and initialize process groups. It works on the module level. The `torch.nn.parallel.DistributedDataParallel()` class is a container that wraps a PyTorch model, allowing it to inherit the functionality of `torch.distributed`. The most common use case involves multiple processes that each operate on their own GPU, either locally or over a network. A process group is initialized to a device using the following code:

```
torch.distributed.init_process_group(backend='nccl', world_size=4,
init_method='...')
```

This is run on each host. The backend specifies what communication protocols to use. The NCCL (pronounced nickel) backend is generally the fastest and most reliable. Be aware that this may need to be installed on your system. The `world_size` is the number of processes in the job and the `init_method` is a URL pointing to location and port for the process to be initialized. This can either be a network address—for example, (`tcp://......`)—or a shared filesystem (`file://... /...`).

A device can be set using `torch.cuda.set_devices(i)`. Finally, we can assign the model by using the code phrase
`model = distributedDataParallel(model, device_ids=[i], output_device=i`. This is typically used in an initialization function that spawns each process and assigns it to a processor. This ensures that every process is coordinated through a master using the same IP address and port.

torch.multiprocessing

The `torch.multiprocessor` package is a replacement for the Python multiprocessor package, and is used in exactly the same way, that is, as a process-based threading interface. One of the ways it extends the Python distributed package is by placing PyTorch tensors into shared memory and only sending their handles to other processes. This is achieved using a `multiprocessing.Queue` object. In general, multiprocessing occurs asynchronously; that is, processes for a particular device are enqueued and executed when the process reaches the top of the queue. Each device executes a process in the order that it is queued and PyTorch periodically synchronizes the multiple processes when copying between devices. This means that, as far as the caller of a multi-process function is concerned, the processes occur synchronously.

One of the major difficulties when writing multithreaded applications is avoiding deadlocking, where two processes compete for a single resource. A common reason for this is when background threads lock or import a module and a subprocess is forked. The subprocess will likely be spawned in a corrupted state, causing a deadlock or another error. The `multiprocessingQueue` class itself spawns multiple background threads to send, receive, and serialize objects, and these threads can also cause deadlocks. For these circumstances, the thread free `multiprocessingQueue.queues.SimpleQueue` can be used.

Optimization techniques

The `torch.optim` package contains a number of optimization algorithms, and each of these algorithms has several parameters that we can use to fine-tune deep learning models. Optimization is a critical component in deep learning, so it is no surprise that different optimization techniques can be key to a model's performance. Remember, its role is to store and update the parameter state based on the calculated gradients of the loss function.

Optimizer algorithms

There are a number of optimization algorithms besides SGD available in PyTorch. The following code shows one such algorithm:

```
optim.Adadelta(params, lr=1.0, rho=0.9, eps=1e-06, weight_decay=0)
```

The `Adedelta` algorithm is based on stochastic gradient descent; however, instead of having the same learning rate over each iteration, the learning rate adapts over time. The `Adadelta` algorithm maintains separate dynamic learning rates for each dimension. This can make training quicker and more efficient, as the overhead of calculating new learning rates on each iteration is quite small compared to actually calculating the gradients. The `Adadelta` algorithm performs well with noisy data for a range of model architectures, large gradients, and in distributed environments. The `Adadelta` algorithm is particularly effective with large models, and works well with large initial learning rates. There are two hyperparameters associated with `Adadelta` that we have not discussed yet. The `rho` is used to calculate the running averages of the squared gradients; this determines the decay rate. The `eps` hyperparameter is added to improve the numerical stability of `Adadelta`, as shown in the following code:

```
optim.Adagrad(params, lr=0.01, lr_decay=0, weight_decay=0,
initial_accumulater_value=0)
```

The `Adagrad` algorithm, or adaptive subgradient methods for stochastic optimization, is a technique that incorporates geometric knowledge of the training data observed in earlier iterations. This allows the algorithm to find infrequent, but highly predictive, features. The `Adagrad` algorithm uses an adaptive learning rate that give frequently occurring features low learning rates and rare features higher learning rates. This has the effect of finding rare but important features of the data and calculating each gradient step accordingly. The learning rate decreases faster over each iteration for more frequent features, and slower for rarer features, meaning that rare features tend to maintain higher learning rates over more iterations. The `Adagrad` algorithm tends to work best for sparse datasets. An example of its application is shown in the following code:

```
optim.Adam(params, lr=0.001, betas(0.9,0.999), eps=1e-08, weight_decay=0,
amsgrad=False)
```

The `Adam` algorithm (adaptive moment estimation) uses an adaptive learning rate based on the mean and the uncentered variance (the first and second moments) of the gradient. Like `Adagrad`, it stores the average of past squared gradients. It also stores the decaying average of these gradients. It calculates the learning rate on each iteration on a per-dimension basis. The `Adam` algorithm combines the benefits of `Adagrad`, working well on sparse gradients, with the ability to work well in online and nonstationary settings. Note that `Adam` takes an optional tuple of beta parameters. These are coefficients that are used in the calculation of the running average and the square of these averages. The `amsgrad` flag, when set to `True`, enables a variant of `Adam` that incorporates the long-term memory of gradients. This can assist with the convergence, where, in certain situations, the standard `Adam` algorithm fails to converge. In addition to the `Adam` algorithm, PyTorch contains two variants of `Adam`. The `optim.SparseAdam` performs lazy updating of parameters, where only the moments that appear in the gradient get updated and applied to the parameters. This provides a more efficient way of working with sparse tensors, such as those used for word embedding. The second variant, `optim.Adamax`, uses the infinite norm to calculate the gradients, and this, theoretically, reduces its susceptibility to noise. In practice, the choice of the best optimizer is often a matter of trial and error.

The following code demonstrates the `optim.RMSprop` optimizer:

```
optim.RMSprop(params, lr=0.01, alpha=0.99, eps=1e-08, weight_decay=0,
momentum=0, centered = False)
```

The `RMSprop` algorithm divides the learning rate for each parameter by a running average of the squares of the magnitude of recent gradients for that particular parameter. This ensures that the step size on each iteration is of the same scale as the gradient. This has the effect of stabilizing gradient descent and reduces the problem of disappearing or exploding gradients. The alpha hyperparameter is a smoothing parameter that helps make the network resilient to noise. Its use can be seen in the following code:

```
optim.Rprop(params, lr=0.01, etas(0.5,1.2), step_sizes(1e_06,50))
```

The `Rprop` algorithm (resilient back propagation) is an adaptive algorithm that calculates weight updates by using the sign, but not the magnitude, of the partial derivative of the cost function for each weight. These are calculated for each weight independently. The `Rprop` algorithm takes a tuple pair of arguments, `etas`. These are multiplicative factors that either increase or decrease the weight depending on the sign of the derivative calculated on the entire loss function of the previous iteration. If the last iteration produced the opposite sign as the current derivative, then the update is multiplied by the first value in the tuple, called `etaminus`, a value less than one and defaulting to `0.5`. If the sign is the same on the current iteration, then that weight update is multiplied by the second value in the `etas` tuple, called `etaplis`, a value greater than `1` and defaulting to `1.2`. In this way, the total error function is minimized.

Learning rate scheduler

The `torch.optim.lr_schedular` class serves as a wrapper around an to schedule the learning rate according to a specific function multiplied by the initial learning rate. The learning rate scheduler can be applied separately to each parameter group. This can speed up training time since, typically, we are able to use larger learning rates at the beginning of the training cycle and shrink this rate as the optimizer approaches minimal loss. Once a scheduler object is defined, it is typically stepped every epoch using `scheduler.step()`. There are a number of learning rate scheduler classes available in PyTorch, and the most common one is shown in the following code:

```
optim.lr_schedular.LambdaLR(optimizer, lr_lambda, last_epoch =-1)
```

This learning rate scheduler class takes a function that multiplies the initial learning rate of each parameter group, and is either passed as a single function or a list of functions if there is more than one parameter group. The `last_epoch` is the index of the last epoch, so the default, `-1`, is the initial learning rate. The following screenshot of an example of this class assumes that we have two parameter groups:

```
1 lamb1 = lambda epoch: 0.9 ** epoch
2 lamb2 = lambda epoch: 0.8 ** epoch
3 schedular = optim.lr_scheduler.LambdaLR optimizer,lr_lambda=[lamb1,lamb2], last_epoch =-1
```

`optim.lr_schedular.StepLR(optimizer, step_size, gamma=0.1, last_epoch=-1` decays the learning rate by a multiplicative factor, gamma, every `step_size` of epochs.

`optim.lr_schedular.MultiStepLR(optimizer, milestones, gamma=0.1,last_epoch=-1)` takes a list of milestones, measured in the number of epochs, when the learning rate is decayed by gamma. The `milestones` phrase is an increasing list of `epoch` indices.

Parameter groups

When an optimizer is instantiated, it is the as well as a variety of hyperparameters such as the learning rate. Optimizers are also passed other hyperparameters specific to each optimization algorithm. It can be extremely useful to set up groups of these hyperparameters, which can be applied to different parts of the model. This can be achieved by creating a parameter group, essentially a list of dictionaries that can be passed to the optimizer.

The `param` variable must either be an iterator over a `torch.tensor` or a Python dictionary specifying a default value of optimization options. Note that the parameters themselves need to be specified as an ordered collection, such as a list, so that parameters are a consistent sequence between model runs.

It is possible to specify the parameters as a parameter group. Consider the code shown in the following screenshot:

```
1 import torch
2 import torch.nn as nn
3 import torch.optim as optim
4
5 w1 = torch.randn(3, 3)
6 w1.requires_grad = True
7 optimizer = optim.SGD([w1], lr=0.1)
8 print(optimizer.param_groups)
[{'params': [tensor([[-1.2673,  1.5080, -0.2775],
        [-0.5443,  0.7693,  0.2868],
        [ 1.3169, -0.4790,  1.6926]])], 'lr': 0.1, 'momentum': 0, 'dampening': 0, 'weight_decay': 0, 'nesterov': False}]
```

The param_groups function returns a list of dictionaries containing the weights and the optimizer hyperparameters. We have already discussed the learning rate. The SGD optimizer also has several other hyperparameters that can be used to fine-tune your models. The momentum hyperparameter modifies the SGD algorithm to help accelerate gradient tensors towards the optimum, usually leading to faster convergence. The momentum defaults to 0; however, using higher values, usually around 0.9, often results in faster optimization. This is especially effective on noisy data. It works by calculating a moving average across the dataset, effectively smoothing the data and consequently improving optimization. The dampening parameter can be used in conjunction with momentum as a dampening factor. The weight_decay parameter applies L2 regularization. This adds a term to the loss function, with the effect of shrinking the parameter estimates, making the model simpler and less likely to overfit. Finally, the nestrove parameter calculates the momentum based on future weight predictions. This enables the algorithm to look ahead by calculating a gradient, not with respect to current parameters, but with respect to approximate future parameters.

We can use the param_groups function to assign different sets of parameters to each parameter group. Consider the code shown in the following screenshot:

```
1  w2 = torch.randn(3, 3)
2  w2.requires_grad = True
3  optimizer.add_param_group({'params': w2})
4  print(optimizer.param_groups)

[{'params': [tensor([[-1.2673,  1.5080, -0.2775],
        [-0.5443,  0.7693,  0.2868],
        [ 1.3169, -0.4790,  1.6926]])], 'lr': 0.1, 'momentum': 0, 'dampening': 0, 'weight_decay': 0, 'nesterov': False}, {'para
ms': [tensor([[ 0.1312,  0.0589, -0.1158],
        [ 1.0284,  0.7809,  0.0052],
        [-0.4003,  0.1439, -1.2612]])], 'lr': 0.1, 'momentum': 0, 'dampening': 0, 'weight_decay': 0, 'nesterov': False}]
```

Here, we have created another weight, w2, and assigned it to a parameter group. Note that in the output we have two sets of hyperparameters, one for each parameter group. This enables us to set weight-specific hyperparameters, allowing, for example, different options to be applied to each layer in a network. We can access each parameter group and change a parameter value, using its list index, as shown in the code in the following screenshot:

```
1  optimizer.param_groups[1]['momentum'] = 0.9
2  print optimizer.param_groups[1]

{'params': [tensor([[ 0.0743,  0.8700,  0.9258],
        [ 0.3472,  0.3480,  0.9883],
        [ 0.3408,  0.8535,  0.1347]])], 'lr': 0.1, 'momentum': 0.9, 'dampening': 0, 'weight_decay': 0, 'nesterov': False}
```

Pretrained models

One of the major difficulties with image classification models is the lack of labeled data. It is difficult to assemble a labeled dataset of sufficient size to train a model well; it is an extremely time consuming and laborious task. This is not such a problem for MNIST, since the images are relatively simple. They are greyscale and largely consist only of target features, there are no distracting background features, and the images are all aligned the same way and are of the same scale. A small dataset of 60,000 images is quite sufficient to train a model well. It is rare to find such a well-organized and consistent dataset in the problems we encounter in real life. Images are often of variable quality, and the target features can be obscured or distorted. They can also be of widely variable scales and rotations. The solution is to use a model architecture that is pretrained on a very large dataset.

PyTorch includes six model architectures based on convolutional networks, designed for working with images on classification or regression tasks. The following list describes these models in detail:

- **AlexNet**: This model is based on convolutional networks and achieves significant performance improvements through a strategy of parallelizing operations across processors. The reason for this is that operations on the convolutional layers are somewhat different to those that occur on the linear layers of a convolutional network. The convolutional layers account for around 90% of the overall computation, but operate on only 55% of the parameters. For the fully connected linear layers, the reverse is true, accounting for around 5% of the computations, yet they contain around 95% of the parameters. AlexNet uses a different parellelizing strategy to take into account the differences between linear and convolutional layers.
- **VGG**: The basic strategy behind **very deep convolutional networks** (VGG) for large-scale image recognition is to increase the depth the number of layers—while using a very small filter with a receptive field of 3 x 3 for all convolutional layers. All hidden layers include ReLU nonlinearity, and the output layers consist of three fully connected linear layers and a softmax layer. The VGG architecture is available in the `vgg11`, `vgg13`, `vgg16`, `vgg19`, `vgg 11_bn`, `vgg13_bn`, `vgg16_bn`, and `vgg19_bn` variants.

- **ResNet**: While very deep networks offer potentially greater computation power, they can be very difficult to optimize and train. Very deep networks often result in gradients that either vanish or explode. ResNet uses a residual network that includes shortcut skip connections to jump over some layers. These skip layers have variable weights so that in the initial training phase the network effectively collapses into a few layers, and as training proceeds, the number of layers is expanded as new features are learned. Resnet is available in the `resnet18`, `resnet34`, `resnet50`, `resnet101`, and `resnet152` variants.

- **SqueezeNet**: SqueezeNet was designed to create smaller models with fewer parameters that are easier to export and run in distributed environments. This is achieved using three strategies. Firstly, it reduces the receptive field of the majority of convolutions from 3 x 3 to 1 X 1. Secondly, it reduces the input channels into the remaining 3 x 3 filters. Thirdly, it down samples in the final layers in the network. SqueezeNet is available in the `squeezenet1_0` and `squeezenet1_1` variants.

- **DenseNet**: Densely convolutional networks—in contrast to standard CNNs, where weights propagate through each layer from input to output— each layer, the feature maps for all preceding layers are used as inputs. This results in shorter connections between layers and a network that encourages the reuse of parameters. This results in fewer parameters and strengthens the propagation of features. DenseNet is available in the `Densenet121`, `Densenet169`, and `Densenet201` variants.

- **Inception**: This architecture uses several strategies to improve performance, including reducing informational bottlenecks by gently reducing dimensionality between the input and output, factorizing convolutions from larger to smaller receptive fields, and balancing the width and depth of the network. The latest version is `inception_v3`. Importantly, Inception requires images to be of size 299 x 299, in contrast to the other models, which require images to be of size 224 x 224.

These models can be initialized with random weights by simply calling their constructor, for example `model = resnet18()`. To initialize a pre-trained model, set the Boolean `pretrained= True`, for example, `model = resnet18(pretrained=True)`. This will load the dataset with their weight values pre-loaded. These weights are calculated by training the network on the `Imagenet` dataset. This dataset contains over 14 million images with over 100 indexes.

Many of these model architectures come in several configurations—for example, `resnet18`, `resnet34`, `vgg11`, and `vgg13`. These variants exploit differences in layer depth, normalization strategies, and other hyperparameters. Finding which one works best for a particular task requires some experimentation.

Also, be aware that these models are designed for working with image data, and require RGB images in the form of `(3, W, H)`. Input images need to be resized to 224 x 224, except for Inception, which requires images of size 299 x 299. Importantly, they need to be normalized in a very specific way. This can be done by creating a `normalize` variable and passing it to `torch.utils.data.DataLoader`, usually as part of a `transforms.compose()` object. It is important that the `normalize` variable is given exactly the following values:

```
normalize=transforms.Normalize(mean=[0.485, 0.456, 0.406], std=[0.229, 0.224, 0.225])
```

This ensures that the input images have the same distribution as the `Imagenet` set that they were trained on.

Implementing a pretrained model

Remember the Guiseppe toys dataset we played with in `Chapter 1`, *Introduction to PyTorch*? We now finally have the tools and knowledge to be able to create a classification model for this data. We are going to do this by using a model pretrained on the `Imagenet` dataset. This is called transfer learning, because we are transferring the learning achieved on one dataset to make predictions on a different, usually much smaller, dataset. Using a network with pretrained weights dramatically increases its performance on much smaller datasets, and this is surprisingly easy to achieve. In the simplest case, we can pass the pretrained model a data of labeled images and simply change the number of output features. Remember that `Imagenet` has `100` indexes or potential labels. For our task here, we want to categorize images into three classes: `toy`, `notoy`, and `scenes`. For this reason, we need to assign the number of output features to three.

The code in the following screenshot is an adaption of code from the transfer learning tutorial by Sasank Chilamkurthy, found at `https://chsasank.github.io`.

To begin, we need to import the data. This is available from this book's website (`.../toydata`). Unzip this file into your working directory. You can actually use any image data you like, provided it has the same directory structure: that is two subdirectories for training and validation sets, and within these two directories, subdirectories for each of the classes. Other datasets you might like to try are the hymenoptera dataset, containing two classes of either ants or bees, available from `https://download.pytorch.org/tutorial/hymenoptera_data.zip`, and the CIFAR-10 dataset from `torchvision/datasets`, or the much larger and more challenging plant seedling dataset, containing 12 classes, available from `https://www.kaggle.com/c/plant-seedlings-classification`.

We need to apply separate data transformations for training and validation datasets, import and make the datasets iterable, and then assign the device to a GPU, if available, as shown in the code in the following screenshot:

```python
data_transforms = {
    'train': transforms.Compose([
        transforms.RandomResizedCrop(224),
        transforms.RandomHorizontalFlip(),
        transforms.ToTensor(),
        transforms.Normalize([0.485, 0.456, 0.406], [0.229, 0.224, 0.225])
    ]),
    'val': transforms.Compose([
        transforms.Resize(256),
        transforms.CenterCrop(224),
        transforms.ToTensor(),
        transforms.Normalize([0.485, 0.456, 0.406], [0.229, 0.224, 0.225])
    ]),
}

data_dir = 'toydata'
image_datasets = {x: datasets.ImageFolder(os.path.join(data_dir, x),
                                           data_transforms[x])
                  for x in ['train', 'val']}
dataloaders = {x: torch.utils.data.DataLoader(image_datasets[x], batch_size=4,
                                              shuffle=True)
               for x in ['train', 'val']}
dataset_sizes = {x: len(image_datasets[x]) for x in ['train', 'val']}
class_names = image_datasets['train'].classes

device = torch.device("cuda:0" if torch.cuda.is_available() else "cpu")
```

Note that a dictionary is used to store two lists of `compose` objects in order to transform the training and validation sets. The `RandomResizedCrop` and `RandomHorizontalFlip` transforms are used to augment the training set. For both the training and validation sets, the images are resized and center cropped, and the specific normalization values, as discussed in the last section, are applied.

The data is unpacked using a dictionary comprehension. This uses the `datasets.Imagefolder` class, which is a generic data loader for use where the data is organized into their class folders. In this case, we have three folders, `NoToy`, `Scenes`, and `SingleToy`, for their respective classes. This directory structure is replicated in both the `val` and `train` directories. There are 117 training images and 24 validation images, divided into the three classes.

We can retrieve the class names simply by calling the `classes` attribute of the `ImageFolder`, as shown in the code in the following screenshot:

```
1 image_datasets['train'].classes

['NoToy', 'Scenes', 'SingleToy']
```

A batch of images and their class indexes can be retrieved using the code in the following screenshot:

```
1 inputs, classes = next(iter(dataloaders['train']))
2 inputs.size

torch.Size([4, 3, 224, 224])
```

The `inputs` tensor has a size in the form of `(batch, RGB, W, H)`. The first tensor, of size 4, contains either a 0 (`NoToy`), 1 (`Scenes`), or 2 (`SingleToy`), representing the class for each of the 4 images in the batch. The class names of each image in the batch can be retrieved using the following list comprehension:

```
1 [class_names[x] for x in classes]

['Scenes', 'SingleToy', 'SingleToy', 'SingleToy']
```

Now, let's look at the function that is used to train the model. This has a similar structure to our earlier training code, with a few additions. Training is divided into two phases, train and val. Also, the learning rate scheduler needs to be stepped for every epoch in the train phase, as shown in the code in the following screenshot:

```
 1  def train_model(model, criterion, optimizer, scheduler, num_epochs=1):
 2      best_model_wts = copy.deepcopy(model.state_dict())
 3      best_acc = 0.0
 4      for epoch in range(num_epochs):
 5          print('Epoch {}/{}'.format(epoch, num_epochs - 1))
 6          for phase in ['train', 'val']:
 7              if phase == 'train':
 8                  scheduler.step()
 9                  model.train()
10              else:
11                  model.eval()
12              running_loss = 0.0
13              running_corrects = 0
14              for inputs, labels in dataloaders[phase]:
15                  inputs = inputs.to(device)
16                  labels = labels.to(device)
17                  optimizer.zero_grad()
18                  with torch.set_grad_enabled(phase == 'train'):
19                      outputs = model(inputs)
20                      _, preds = torch.max(outputs, 1)
21                      loss = criterion(outputs, labels)
22                      if phase == 'train':
23                          loss.backward()
24                          optimizer.step()
25                  running_loss += loss.item() * inputs.size(0)
26                  running_corrects += torch.sum(preds == labels.data)
27              epoch_loss = running_loss / dataset_sizes[phase]
28              epoch_acc = running_corrects.double() / dataset_sizes[phase]
29              print('{} Loss: {:.4f} Acc: {:.4f}'.format(
30                  phase, epoch_loss, epoch_acc))
31              if phase == 'val' and epoch_acc > best_acc:
32                  best_acc = epoch_acc
33                  best_model_wts = copy.deepcopy(model.state_dict())
34          print()
35      print('Best val Acc: {:4f}'.format(best_acc))
36      model.load_state_dict(best_model_wts)
37      return model
```

The `train_model` function takes as arguments the model, the loss criteria, a learning rate scheduler, and the number of epochs. The model weights are stored by deep copying `model.state_dict()`. Deep copying this ensures that all elements of the state dictionary are copied, and not just referenced, into the `best_model_wts` variable. For every epoch there are two phases, a training phase and a validation phase. In the validation phase, the model is set to evaluation mode using `model.eval()`. This changes the behaviour of some model layers, typically the dropout layer, setting the dropout probability to zero to validate on the complete model. The accuracy and loss for both the training and validation phases are printed on each epoch. Once this is done, the best validation accuracy is printed.

Before we can run the training code, we need to instantiate the model and set up the optimizer, loss criteria, and learning rate scheduler. Here, we use the `resnet18` model, as shown in the code in the following screenshot. This code works for all `resnet` variants, although not necessarily with the same accuracy:

```
1  model = models.resnet50(pretrained=True)
2  num_ftrs = model_ft.fc.in_features
3  model.fc = nn.Linear(num_ftrs, 3)
4  model = model_ft.to(device)
5  criterion = nn.CrossEntropyLoss()
6  optimizer_ft = optim.SGD(model_ft.parameters(), lr=0.001, momentum=0.9)
7  exp_lr_scheduler = lr_scheduler.StepLR(optimizer_ft, step_size=7, gamma=0.1)
8  now=time.time()
9  model = train_model(model_ft, criterion, optimizer_ft, exp_lr_scheduler,
10                      num_epochs=22)
```

The model is used with all weights, excluding the output layer, trained on the `Imagenet` dataset. We need only change the output layer since the weights in all hidden layers are frozen in their pretrained state. This is done by setting the output layer to a linear layer with its output set to the number of classes we are predicting. The output layer is essentially a feature extractor for the dataset we are working with. At the output, the features we are trying to extract are the classes themselves.

We can look at the structure of the model by simply running `print(model)`. The final layer is named `fc`, so we can access this layer with `model.fc`. This is assigned a linear layer and is passed the number of input features, accessed with `fc.in_features`, and the number of output classes, here set to 3. When we run this model, we are able to achieve an accuracy of around 90%, which is actually quite impressive, considering the tiny dataset we are using. This is possible because most of the training, apart from the final layer, is done on a much larger training set.

It is possible, and a worthwhile exercise, to use the other pretrained models with a few changes to the training code. For example, the DenseNet model can be directly substituted for ResNet by simply changing the name of the output layer from `fc` to `classifier`, so instead of writing `model.fc`, we write `model.classifier`. SqueezeNet, VGG, and AlexNet have their final layers wrapped inside a sequential container, so to change the output `fc` layer, we need to go through the following four steps:

1. Find the number of filters in the output layer
2. Convert the layers in the sequential object to a list and remove the last element
3. Add the last linear layer, specifying the number of output classes, to the end of the list
4. Convert the list back to a sequential container and add it to the model class

For the `vgg11` model, the following code can be used to implement these four steps:

```
1  num_ftrs = model_vgg.classifier[6].in_features
2  features = list(model_vgg.classifier.children())[:-1]
3  features.extend([nn.Linear(num_ftrs, 3)])
4  model_vgg.classifier = nn.Sequential(*features)
```

Summary

Now that you have an understanding of the foundations of deep learning, you should be well placed to apply this knowledge to specific learning problems that you are interested in. In this chapter, we have developed an out-of-the-box solution for image classification using pretrained models. As you have seen, this is quite simple to implement, and can be applied to almost any image classification problem you can think of. Of course, the actual performance in each situation will depend on the number and quality of images presented, as well as the precise tuning of the hyperparameters associated with each model and task.

You can generally get very good results on most image classification tasks by simply running the pretrained models with default parameters. This requires no theoretical knowledge, apart from installing the programs' running environment. You will find that when you adjust some parameters, you may improve the network's training time and/or accuracy. For example, you may have noticed that increasing the learning rate may dramatically improve a model's performance over a small number of epochs, but over subsequent epochs the accuracy actually declines. This is an example of gradient descent overshooting, and failing to find the true optimum. Finding the best learning rate requires some knowledge of gradient descent.

In order to get the most out of PyTorch and apply it in different problem domains—such as language processing, physical modeling, weather and climate prediction, and so on (the applications are almost endless)—you need to have some understanding of the theory behind these algorithms. This not only allows improvement on known tasks, such as image classification, but also gives you some insight into how deep learning might be applied in a situation where, for example, the input data is a time series and the task is to predict the next sequence. After reading this book, you should know the solution, which is of course to use a recurrent network. You would have noticed that the model we built to generate text—that is, to make predictions on a sequence—was quite different to the model used to make predictions on static image data. But what about the model you would have to build to help you gain insights into a particular process? This could be the electronic traffic on a website, the physical traffic on a road network, the carbon and oxygen cycle of the planet, or a human biological system. These are the frontiers of deep learning, with immense power to do good. I hope reading this short introduction has left you feeling empowered and inspired to begin exploring some of these applications.

Other Books You May Enjoy

If you enjoyed this book, you may be interested in these other books by Packt:

Deep Learning with PyTorch
Vishnu Subramanian

ISBN: 978-1-78862-433-6

- Use PyTorch for GPU-accelerated tensor computations
- Build custom datasets and data loaders for images and test the models using torchvision and torchtext
- Build an image classifier by implementing CNN architectures using PyTorch
- Build systems that do text classification and language modeling using RNN, LSTM, and GRU
- Learn advanced CNN architectures such as ResNet, Inception, Densenet, and learn how to use them for transfer learning
- Learn how to mix multiple models for a powerful ensemble model
- Generate new images using GANs and generate artistic images using style transfer

TensorFlow Machine Learning Cookbook - Second Edition
Nick McClure

ISBN: 978-1-78913-168-0

- Become familiar with the basic features of the TensorFlow library
- Get to know Linear Regression techniques with TensorFlow
- Learn SVMs with hands-on recipes
- Implement neural networks to improve predictive modeling
- Apply NLP and sentiment analysis to your data
- Master CNN and RNN through practical recipes
- Implement the gradient boosted random forest to predict housing prices
- Take TensorFlow into production

Leave a review - let other readers know what you think

Please share your thoughts on this book with others by leaving a review on the site that you bought it from. If you purchased the book from Amazon, please leave us an honest review on this book's Amazon page. This is vital so that other potential readers can see and use your unbiased opinion to make purchasing decisions, we can understand what our customers think about our products, and our authors can see your feedback on the title that they have worked with Packt to create. It will only take a few minutes of your time, but is valuable to other potential customers, our authors, and Packt. Thank you!

Index

A

activation functions 72, 73
agent 37
AlexNet 129
Amazon Web Services (AWS) 14
Anaconda distribution, of Python
  reference 10
artificial neural networks (ANNs)
  about 55
  perceptron 56, 57, 58
autograd package
  about 62, 63, 64
  computational graph 64, 65

B

backpropagation 55
basic PyTorch operations
  about 14, 15
  default value initialization 15, 16
  in place operations 21, 22
  indexing 19
  NumPy array, converting to tensors 16
  reshaping 20
  slicing 19
  tensor, converting to NumPy array 17
batch gradient descent (BGD) 49
batch normalization
  about 96, 97
  reference 96
benchmarking models 83, 84, 85, 86, 87
binary classification 37
binary cross-entropy loss 71

C

categories
  handling 40

central processing unit (CPU) 120
classification
  about 37
  binary classification 37
  multi-label classification 38
  multiple output classification 38
classifier
  evaluating 38, 39
cloud server hosts
  Amazon Web Services (AWS) 14
  Digital Ocean 12
clustering 36
computational graph 64, 65
convolution kernel 88
convolutional networks
  about 88
  multiple convolutional layers 91
  single convolutional layer 88, 89, 90
cost function 46

D

data
  loading 22, 23
datasets
  concatenating 31
default value initialization 15, 16
dense word embedding 41
Digital Ocean
  about 12
  droplet setup 12
  reference 12
dimensionality reduction 36
distributed environments
  about 119, 122
  torch.distributed 122
  torch.multiprocessing 123

F

feature map 88
feature scaling
  min-max scaling 40
  normalization 40
  standardization 40
  techniques 40
feature vector 50
features 39
filter 88

G

gated recurrent unit
  language model, building 111, 113, 115, 116,
    117
gradient descent 47, 48
graphical processing units (GPUs)
  about 9
  using 120, 121

H

hymenoptera dataset
  reference 132
hyperparameter 48, 81, 82, 83
hypothesis function 45

I

ImageFolder 30
in place operations 21
Inception 130
indexing 19
internal co-variate shift (ICS) 96
IPython
  about 13
  tunneling in to 13

J

just in time (JIT) C++ compiler 10

K

k-means 36

L

learning rate 48
learning rate scheduler 126, 127
learning tasks
  supervised learning 35
  unsupervised learning 35
linear algebra 41
linear models
  about 45, 65
  activation functions 72, 73
  gradient descent 47, 48
  linear regression 65, 66, 68, 69
  logistic regression 70, 71, 72
  multiple features 50
  normal equation 51
  saving 69
logistic regression 51, 53, 54
long short-term memory networks (LSTMS)
  about 107, 109, 110
  implementing 110, 111
  language model, building with gated recurrent
    unit 111, 113, 115, 116, 117

M

machine learning
  approaches 34, 35
matrix
  about 42
  example 43, 44, 45
mean squared error (MSE) 46
models
  about 41
  linear models 45
multi-class classification
  example 73, 74, 75, 76, 77, 78
multi-label classification 38
multilayered networks 81, 82, 83
multiple convolutional layers
  about 91
  multiple-layer CNN, building 94, 95, 96
  pooling layers 91, 92
  single-layer CNN, building 92, 93, 94
multiple features 50
multiple kernels 90, 91

multiple output classification 38
multiple-layer CNN
  batch normalization 96, 97
  building 94, 95, 96
multiprocessor
  about 119
  graphical processing units (GPUs), using 120, 121

N

nonlinear models 54, 55
normal equation 51
NumPy arrays
  converting, to tensors 16

O

Open Neural Network Exchange (ONNX) 9
optimization techniques
  about 124
  learning rate scheduler 126, 127
  parameter groups 128
optimizer algorithms 124, 125, 126

P

parameter groups 128
parameter vector 50
plant seedling dataset
  reference 132
pretrained model
  about 129, 130, 131
  AlexNet 129
  DenseNet 130
  implementing 131, 133, 135, 136
  Inception 130
  ResNet 130
  SqueezeNet 130
  very deep convolutional networks (VGG) 129
principle component analysis (PCA) 36
PyTorch dataset loaders
  about 24
  custom dataset, creating 27, 29
  DataLoader 26
  image, loading 26
  transforms 29
PyTorch

about 8
advantage 9
characteristics 10
installing 10
reference 11

R

receptive field 88
rectified linear unit (ReLU) 73
recurrent artificial neurons (RANs) 100, 101
recurrent networks
  about 99
  implementing 101, 102, 103, 104, 105, 106, 107
reinforcement learning 37
reshaping 19
ResNet 130

S

single convolutional layer
  about 88, 89, 90
  multiple kernels 90, 91
single-layer CNN
  building 92, 93, 94
slicing 19
Spyder 11
SqueezeNet 130
stochastic gradient descent (SGD) 49
stores
  perceptron 59
supervised learning
  about 35, 37
  classification 37

T

tape-based auto-diif 9
tensor
  converting, to NumPy array 17
text
  handling 40
torch.distributed 122
torch.multiprocessing 123

U

unit 55
unsupervised learning
  about 35, 36
  clustering 36
  principle component analysis (PCA) 36

reinforcement learning 37

V

valid padding 89
vdumoulin's excellent animations
  reference 91
very deep convolutional networks (VGG) 129